How to Create an Organic Aquarium

The Beginner's Guide to Soil-Based Freshwater Aquariums

OLIVER JAMIESON

ACRE PRESS
an imprint of
Egg Publishing

ACRE PRESS
An imprint of
Egg Publishing
eggpublishing.com

First published 2025
001
Copyright © Oliver Jamieson, 2025
The moral right of the author has been asserted

All rights reserved
The permission under 'Epigraph' on page 213 constitutes an extension of this copyright page
Please note that the information contained within this publication is for educational and entertainment purposes only. Whilst the publisher has made every reasonable effort to ensure the information presented is accurate and complete, no liability can be accepted for any loss incurred in any way whatsoever by any person acting, or refraining to act, as a result of reading the information contained herein.

All images copyright © Egg Publishing 2025

Edited by Sophie Judge
Proofread by Lisa Stephen (Eagle Editing)
Interior design by Wendy Mach (White Stone Pages)
Cover design by Wendy Mach (White Stone Pages)
Illustrations by Cahyani G. Mulwinda

A catalogue record for this book is available from the National Library of Australia

ISBN: 978-1-763-71379-6 (Hardback)
ISBN: 978-1-763-71377-2 (Paperback)
ISBN: 978-1-763-71378-9 (eBook)

hello@eggpublishing.com

Spring becomes stream becomes river, and all three seek the sea.

Robert Macfarlane (2025)

Contents

Introduction
What is an organic aquarium? 1
Where did this approach come from? 3
What am I getting myself into? 3

The Principles of an Organic Aquarium
The anatomy of an organic aquarium 5
The three objectives of an organic aquarium 6
Bringing it all together 13

Equipment
What type of aquarium should I get? 15
How to decide 19
How do I light my aquarium? 20
How do I keep the water moving? 22
Do I need to heat It? 23
Can I decorate it with rocks or driftwood… or a dinosaur skull? ...24
What do I need to keep my aquarium clean? 27
Where do I get everything from? 29

Water
Can I use tap water? 33
How do I test the water? 33

Substrate
What kind of soil can I use? 39
How do I prepare the soil? 42
What do I use for the cap? 43

How deep should the substrate be? 44
How long will the soil last? 45
Will soil make my aquarium water yellow?.....................46

Plants
Which plants should I get? 49
How many plants should I get? 51
Do I need to fertilise my plants? 53
How are plants sold? 54
How do I know if I'm buying a healthy plant? 55
Can I grow houseplants from my aquarium? 56

Animals
When can I add fish and invertebrates?.......................59
Which species can I keep? 63
How many should I add? 65
How do I introduce microfauna? 66
Protecting microfauna with botanicals 66
How do I add animals safely? 67
What should I feed them? 68

Setting Up Your Aquarium
Shopping list 71
The prep 73
The build 76
The balance 81

Maintenance
How do I maintain an organic aquarium? 85
Daily and weekly tasks 85

Monthly and quarterly tasks 86
What if I don't know what to do? 87

Conclusion
A growing community 89

How-to Guides
Culturing wild microfauna 92
Adding botanicals to your aquarium 94
Blanching spinach as a supplement 96

Field Guide
Plants 100
    Floating plants 103
    Root-feeding plants 117
    Water column feeders...................................131
    Epiphytes and mosses...................................145
Animals 159
    Fish 161
    Invertebrates..191
    Microfauna...205

Notes
Bibliography 213
Resources 215
Unit conversions 219

Acknowledgements
Contributors 223
About the author 225

Units of measurement: Throughout this book, metric units are used to ensure clarity and consistency for a broad international audience. For readers more familiar with imperial measurements, a conversion table is provided at the back of the book.

An exception has been made for aquarium volumes, which are given in US gallons. This convention aligns with common practice in the aquarium hobby and typically results in rounder, more recognisable figures than litre conversions.

A note on sponsors: Some products mentioned in this book are associated with sponsors. These sponsorship arrangements help offset the costs of creating resources like this book, but they have not influenced the content or recommendations. The author only endorses companies whose products are genuinely used, trusted, and align with the approach presented.

Introduction

Introduction

WHAT IS AN ORGANIC AQUARIUM?

An organic aquarium is an ecosystem. It is a rich community of living organisms – flora, fauna, and fungi – all at work in their tiny worlds. If you have ever wanted to bring a slice of nature indoors, you're in the right place.

But bringing the outside inside is easier said than done. Planning your first aquarium is bewildering, especially when online forums, YouTube channels, and books offer seemingly contradictory advice. It appears daunting, but it shouldn't.

This confusion exists because multiple paths lead to the same destination – a healthy ecosystem. Each method is valid, just with different goals the aquarist (that's you!) may have.

As you have chosen this book, you will likely identify with one or more of the below:
- You are a beginner, and you want to learn a simple way of growing plants and keeping fish.
- You want an affordable method so that you can explore this new hobby without lots of upfront costs.
- You would like a quiet, low-maintenance aquarium – something calming and not too time consuming.
- You are interested in creating an ecosystem and want to observe how it evolves and stabilises with time.

With the above in mind, the answer is clear. The organic aquarium method is the simplest, cheapest, and most rewarding option available to you.

It is the simplest as it has the fewest moving parts and requires significantly less maintenance than a conventional aquarium. It is the cheapest as it is built using easily sourced materials and does not require specialist equipment to work. And it is the most rewarding option as the result is a dynamic ecosystem. A little world brought indoors.

So, what goes into an organic aquarium? An organic aquarium consists of aquatic plants, a substrate made of garden soil and a layer of sand or gravel, and a thriving colony of microbes. When combined, the result is an ecosystem that requires minimal intervention. The soil supports healthy plant growth, and the healthy plants keep the water clean. In comparison, a conventional freshwater aquarium has an inert substrate (meaning zero nutrients), so synthetic nutrient-rich fertilisers are necessary to grow plants in these setups, and an aquarium filter is a must to keep the water clean.

If you have already started exploring soil-based aquariums, you may have encountered terms such as: the **Walstad Method**, the **Father Fish Method**, **Dirted Tanks**, **Natural Planted Tanks**, and **Ecosystem Tanks**. These approaches are all similar in concept, just with certain distinguishing features. In this book, we will be using 'organic aquarium' as an umbrella term for low-tech, soil-based planted aquariums. The term 'organic' doesn't signify an absolute rejection of synthetic materials or additives. Rather it acknowledges and celebrates the web of biological interactions that drive this approach. The plants, the soil, and the microbes run the show.

We should also define low-tech. In the aquarium hobby, low-tech means that there is no carbon dioxide injection and no high-intensity lighting (used together to accelerate plant growth). A low-tech aquarium typically has low-intensity lighting, and it relies on simple equipment and natural processes for healthy (albeit slower) plant growth. An organic aquarium is a low-tech system.

Introduction

WHERE DID THIS APPROACH COME FROM?

Diana Walstad pioneered the scientific foundation for this method in her groundbreaking book, *Ecology of the Planted Aquarium*. Whilst the use of soil as an aquarium substrate existed before her publication, Walstad's research explained why these systems worked, documenting the biological interactions that allow plants and microbes to replace mechanical filtration. Her work transformed what was considered an unconventional, unreliable approach into a scientifically supported methodology.

While this book covers all the practical tools necessary for success, readers interested in the deeper scientific mechanisms should consider Walstad's text an invaluable companion resource. This book focuses on translating complex biology into straightforward techniques that work for beginners. Think of it as the field guide to Walstad's scientific treatise: where she provides the theoretical framework, this text offers the hands-on instructions.

WHAT AM I GETTING MYSELF INTO?

Of course, every method has its trade-offs, and the organic approach isn't for everyone. More so than other approaches, an organic aquarium requires trust in natural processes. At the start of your aquarium's life you will have to resist the urge to intervene. You are giving your ecosystem time to find its own balance, which can mean a few unpredictable weeks. For hobbyists who value fast results or more control, this slower, ecosystem-based method might feel frustrating. But if you enjoy learning through observation, this method rewards curiosity and patience.

And while the maintenance is much less than a conventional aquarium, it doesn't mean zero maintenance. You'll still need to feed your animals, trim your plants, and do the occasional water change. The difference is that you're working *with* the system rather than trying to control it.

If you are willing to trade some initial predictability for long-term stability, the result is a place where animals, plants, soil, and microbes form an intricate web of life.

1

The Principles of an Organic Aquarium

THE ANATOMY OF AN ORGANIC AQUARIUM

An organic aquarium is an aquatic ecosystem powered by natural processes. At its core is a living substrate (garden soil capped with sand or gravel) which supports plant life and a microbial community. In this ecosystem, plants filter the water and use waste to grow, while microbes break down organic matter and release nutrients for the plants.

Lighting is moderate and timed to support photosynthesis in sync with natural carbon dioxide levels, and gentle water movement ensures an even distribution of oxygen and nutrients. Temperature is stable and matched to the needs of the tank's inhabitants to support biological function.

Every component is chosen to support the system's natural rhythms, creating a balanced, dynamic environment where plants, animals, and microbes work together to maintain ecosystem health.

THE THREE OBJECTIVES OF AN ORGANIC AQUARIUM

The first question beginners ask is: 'How does the water stay clean?' In a conventional, high-tech setup, the aquarist relies on the aquarium filter. The filter cleans the water using two methods: biological filtration and mechanical filtration.

For **biological filtration**, the filter houses a special type of bacteria that consumes pollutants and converts them into less toxic substances. For **mechanical filtration**, it has filter media (e.g. floss, sponges, foam blocks) which physically trap fish waste, uneaten food, and decaying plant matter (detritus, often referred to as mulm). Filtration is centralised within the filter.

In an organic aquarium, filtration is decentralised. It is the living network of plants and microbes spread throughout the tank. To build a healthy organic aquarium, we need to achieve three objectives:

1. Create a decentralised biological filter
2. Replace mechanical filtration with the detritus crew
3. Keep the plants and microbes happy.

OBJECTIVE 1: CREATE A DECENTRALISED BIOLOGICAL FILTER

Aquarium plants are biological filters.

In a conventional aquarium, the nitrogen cycle is in command: fish waste and decomposing matter produce ammonia (toxic); nitrifying bacteria housed in the filter convert ammonia into nitrite (also toxic); then to nitrate (much less toxic); lastly, the aquarist removes nitrate weekly via water changes before too much of the substance accumulates.

In an organic aquarium, the beginning is the same: fish waste and decomposing matter produce ammonia; but then the plants absorb it. The plants act quickly to absorb ammonia and combine it with hydrogen to create non-toxic ammonium[1], which they need to grow.

As the plant grows, it locks the nitrogen from ammonia/ammonium and other nutrients into living tissue (in new leaves, stems, and roots), effectively removing toxins from circulation. This strategy creates stability by storing nutrients in biomass, rather than leaving them as free-floating ions that fuel algae or require manual removal[2]. In low-tech terms, plant growth and pruning perform a similar role to a water change: it removes waste but only after that waste has been turned into something productive – plant growth.

So, in building an organic aquarium, we want to find the critical plant mass as early as possible. That means matching the number of plants to the amount of ammonia being produced before trouble brews. Ammonia is the most toxic form of nitrogen in an aquarium; if plants consume it right away, that's cleaner water for your fish, and more plant growth for you to enjoy. Nice.

OBJECTIVE 2: REPLACE MECHANICAL FILTRATION WITH THE DETRITUS CREW

How can we remove fish waste, uneaten food, and decaying plant matter without an aquarium filter there to trap it? It's simple – we don't want to. When an aquarist removes detritus from the system, they short-circuit the detritus cycle, inadvertently cutting out a beneficial web of life[3].

The detritus cycle, or more accurately, the detrital food web is the network of organisms that eat detritus and, in turn, become food for others[4]. Within this food web there is a whole community of detritivores (critters that consume detritus) and decomposers (bacteria and fungi that chemically break it down) that process waste. Their continuous activity is central to the organic method as decomposition unlocks nutrients in the soil and in the detritus as simpler compounds that plants can use.

By keeping the nutrients from detritus actively circulating inside the aquarium, we reduce the need for intervention (like dosing fertilisers, syphoning substrate, and performing water changes). With an active detritus crew, every time you feed your fish, you add nutrients to the system that plants will eventually use. Any portion of the food that goes uneaten or passes through as waste becomes detritus, entering the cycle and fuelling the system.

Contrast this with a conventional tank where the inert substrate can cause problems. These substrates cannot sustain a detrital food web, and without an active detritus cycle, waste that gathers can rot and foul the water unless the aquarist frequently removes it. The result is a toxic substrate. A detrital food web, however, needs organic matter. It relies on decaying organics, and it welcomes more. These organisms stop detritus from smothering the substrate by constantly churning and processing it. This bioturbation (natural stirring of substrate) ensures that waste is continually mixed and oxygenated, eventually becoming plant food rather than accumulating and polluting the water.

The smallest members of the detrital food web are bacteria and fungi. These microbes are already at work in your soil. They start the breakdown process by decomposing organic compounds, essentially pre-digesting waste. Slightly larger are microorganisms like protozoa and rotifers that feed on the bacteria and tiny bits of detritus. Larger still, you have nematodes (tiny worms), and oligochaete worms (slightly larger than nematodes), that feed on protozoa. As well as detritivores like copepods (tiny crustaceans), ostracods (seed-shaped tiny crustaceans), and amphipods (slightly larger tiny crustaceans), which multiply in planted tanks. These larger detritovores often arrive in your aquarium as hitchhikers attached to aquatic plants. Far from being pests, these critters – known collectively as microfauna – are an essential part of the clean-up crew, and their constant grazing helps keep the nutrients cycling. Each member of the detrital food web contributes to breaking down organic compounds – in the soil and in the detritus – into smaller and smaller pieces, until what's left are basic nutrients plants can absorb.

Importantly, the presence of small invertebrates like worms, copepods, and ostracods – in quantity and variety – is a strong indicator that your system is thriving. Just like in your garden soil, these tiny critters are signs of a rich, functioning ecosystem[5]. If they're multiplying in your tank, it means your microbial communities are healthy and food webs are actively supporting nutrient recycling. By encouraging these helpers, we create an ecosystem.

OBJECTIVE 3: KEEP THE PLANTS AND MICROBES HAPPY

If plants are doing the biological filtering, and the microbes are doing the mechanical filtering, why do we need soil? Soil fuels the system. It provides plants with the carbon dioxide needed for growth, and it provides a habitat for the detritus crew who keep nutrients cycling.

Soil keeps plants happy

NUTRIENTS

In a conventional aquarium, the substrate serves two purposes: it forms the aesthetic foundation of the tank, allowing the aquarist to cover the tank's floor and shape a landscape within the aquarium; and it acts as a planting medium, anchoring plants in place. A gravel substrate is, however, inert. It does not provide nutrients to the plants, so synthetic fertilisers are necessary to keep plants alive.

In an organic aquarium, the substrate serves a third purpose: the soil contains a buffet of nutrients (e.g. nitrogen, phosphorus, potassium, iron, and more). These compounds are bound up in minerals and organic matter (e.g. decomposing twigs and leaves), and they slowly become available to plant roots as microbes in the soil break these compounds down (known as mineralising). Unlike liquid fertilisers, which spike the nutrient levels in the water column all at once, soil offers a slow-release fertilisation scheme[6].

CARBON

Carbon provides energy and building material for organisms. When we talk about carbon in the aquarium hobby, we are referring to carbon dioxide. The challenge is ensuring plants have enough carbon dioxide for growth. Remember photosynthesis from school? Carbon dioxide plus water plus light equals plant growth. This is why the production of carbon dioxide is essential in planted aquariums.

As we established earlier, an organic aquarium is a low-tech system. So how do we get enough carbon for the plants without carbon dioxide injection? Carbon enters the system through the atmosphere (more on that later) and through decomposition in the soil. The organics in the soil release carbon dioxide as microbes decompose them.

Combined, these carbon sources sustain plant growth without needing high-tech interventions like carbon dioxide injections or liquid fertilisers. It's important to note that natural carbon dioxide production is modest, so we tailor our lighting and plant choices around it (more on this later too)[7].

Soil keeps microbes happy

Without its decomposers, an organic aquarium will fail. Thankfully, good soil is alive. And by using it as a substrate, we seed the tank with beneficial microbes and provide a vast surface area to keep our detrital crew healthy and active[8]. The soil substrate creates a gradient of conditions that can be categorised in two distinct zones:

- Aerobic (oxygen-rich) zones: Found at the soil's surface, these areas host bacteria that quickly defuse harmful substances like ammonia and hydrogen sulphide before they reach the water column.
- Anaerobic (oxygen-poor) zones: Deeper layers of the soil, where oxygen is limited, provide a habitat for specialised bacteria that decompose organic material, releasing

nutrients like iron, phosphorus, and carbon dioxide that plants absorb directly.

A healthy organic aquarium does not have soil that's either fully aerobic or anaerobic – it has zones of both in the substrate. Think of Goldilocks: if the soil becomes too aerobic, vital nutrients will be locked away in forms plants cannot use; if it becomes too anaerobic, the soil will produce hydrogen sulphide and an oversupply of ammonia (both are toxic to aquatic life). An organic aquarium uses three techniques to find the right balance: **soil depth**, **cap depth**, and **rooted plants**.

SOIL DEPTH

A soil depth of 2–4 cm creates a natural oxygen gradient: aerobic at the surface and increasingly anaerobic deeper down. This supports different microbial communities at different layers: aerobic bacteria near the surface handle detritus, while anaerobic bacteria deeper down help with decomposition. Shallower than 2 cm, and you lose the beneficial anaerobic zones; deeper than 4 cm, and the beneficial aerobic zones will be overwhelmed by the deeper anaerobic zones.

CAP DEPTH

The soil shouldn't sit exposed at the bottom of the tank; there is a 2.5–4 cm deep upper layer of coarse sand or fine gravel known as the 'cap'. The cap plays two key roles: one structural, one chemical. First, the cap provides physical stability. It keeps the soil in place, preventing cloudy water and controlling nutrient release. Second, the cap creates an 'oxidised microzone': a thin, oxygen-rich safety net where aerobic bacteria convert rising ammonia and hydrogen sulphide into less harmful forms before they reach the water column[9]. As the cap is more porous than the soil beneath, water can gently travel through it. This oxygenates the upper layer of the soil, supporting aerobic bacteria. The cap is a breathable barrier.

ROOTED PLANTS

Plants are your strongest allies in protecting the natural balance beneath the surface. As roots grow, they transport oxygen from the leaves down into the substrate, releasing it in tiny amounts into the soil (an area surrounding the root known as the rhizosphere). These oxygen-rich microzones are vital habitats for aerobic bacteria. Plant roots essentially farm beneficial microbes, nurturing them to create the ideal conditions within the substrate[10]. In this system, the bacteria and the plants work together, with plant roots oxygenating the soil and hosting beneficial microbes, while the microbes, in turn, unlock nutrients that support plant growth[11].

Dense planting right from the start of your aquarium's life ensures roots quickly permeate the soil, keeping it balanced and healthy.

Over time, these three techniques build a rich, biologically active substrate that nourishes plants and microbes. With a buffet at their roots, your plants are well equipped to outcompete algae, support water stability, and drive the entire ecosystem forward.

A note on stagnant water

Stagnation is when a body of water stops moving and gradually becomes toxic to aquatic life. When there is no movement in your aquarium, you increase the likelihood of a buildup of biofilm (a natural layer made of bacteria and organic matter) on the water's surface. This biofilm acts as a barrier, blocking gas exchange. When this happens, atmospheric oxygen cannot enter the water, and carbon dioxide cannot escape. Stagnation suffocates the ecosystem.

In a conventional setup, the aquarium filter combats stagnation by circulating water and disrupting biofilm so gas exchange can occur. Decentralising filtration doesn't mean we can ignore this role. An organic aquarium still needs water movement, but it is gentler than a conventional system.

The Principles of an Organic Aquarium

In tanks under 20 gallons, the activity of your animals and natural convection currents (movement caused by changes in temperature) are often enough to prevent stagnation. In larger tanks, we achieve this gentle circulation with an undersized internal filter or small submersible water pump positioned below the water line.

Whilst it is expected to have some biofilm across your water's surface (and it is beneficial to have it elsewhere in your tank), it is important to make sure it doesn't take over. If the water surface begins to look thick and oily, it is likely impacting gas exchange. With a bit of experimentation, you can find a height for your filter or pump that agitates the water's surface enough to prevent biofilm, whilst maintaining a healthy level of gas exchange.

Having said that, it is important to avoid disrupting the water surface too much. Surface agitation increases gas exchange; this is good for bringing more oxygen into the system – which keeps plants and animals happy and supports beneficial aerobic decomposition – but it causes valuable carbon dioxide to escape before plants can use it[12]. For this reason, air stones and hang-on-back (HOB) filters are not recommended in an organic aquarium. Both constantly disturb the water's surface, which undermines the delicate gas balance of a low-tech planted tank. Instead, we just want the water in motion. This gives plants more contact time with nutrients in the water column, while keeping gas exchange at a healthy level.

BRINGING IT ALL TOGETHER

An organic aquarium is a decentralised, living system. If you create a strong foundation and give your aquarium time to organise itself, the result is a stable, resilient ecosystem.

You don't have to memorise every detail. If you understand these three main objectives – plants as filters, microbes as cleaners, and soil as fuel – you're already ahead of the game.

So what do you need to get started?

2

Equipment

WHAT TYPE OF AQUARIUM SHOULD I GET?

CHOOSING THE RIGHT MATERIAL

When purchasing your first aquarium, you'll need to decide between glass and acrylic. While both can support a healthy organic system, glass is generally the better choice.

Glass is more expensive than acrylic, but it is more scratch-resistant, easier to clean, and maintains its clarity. Cleaning tools like plastic bank or gift cards or razor blade scrapers can be used safely on glass, but even gentle cleaning can leave marks on acrylic.

Make sure that your tank has a foam layer underneath. Tanks are often supplied with these attached, but if not, you will need to source one to match your aquarium's size. The foam layer is essential as it distributes the weight of the aquarium evenly and prevents any pressure points from cracking the bottom of the tank.

CHOOSING THE RIGHT SIZE

The 'correct' aquarium size depends on your space, budget, and how you want to engage with your system. If you rent your home, check with your landlord to see if there are aquarium size limits in place – that may make the decision for you.

NANO AND SMALL TANKS: UNDER 20 GALLONS

From a practical standpoint, nano tanks (under 10 gallons) and small tanks (under 20 gallons) are more accessible. They take up little room, making them a great option for apartments, student housing, or home offices.

Tanks under 20 gallons are also much more affordable. The tank is cheaper, but you also use less substrate, fewer plants, and the general upkeep can be done quickly with minimal equipment. If a problem arises, it's easier to respond fast; for example, a 50% water change takes just a bucket and 10 minutes of your time.

That said, smaller doesn't always mean easier. While some maintenance is reduced, plant growth needs more frequent attention – trimming, thinning, and replanting schedules are more tightly packed.

Tank size also limits the number of animals you can keep. In an organic aquarium under 10 gallons, you'll need to stock lightly, typically a shrimp-only setup. Larger species or mixed communities will exceed the system's ability to process waste.

The limited water volume in smaller tanks also means parameters fluctuate faster in response to feeding, evaporation, or changes in temperature and water chemistry. This quickly builds an understanding of aquarium dynamics, but it also means the system is less forgiving. A small mistake, like overfeeding or inconsistent lighting, can cause visible imbalances, and without regular attention, your aquarium's water parameters could swing out of control.

Small tanks reward attentiveness. They suit people who enjoy frequent interaction and want to develop their skills through trial, error, and close observation.

MEDIUM AND LARGE TANKS: 20 GALLONS AND OVER

Larger tanks require more space and upfront investment (especially when sourcing enough plants), but they offer greater stability once established. With a larger volume of water, fluctuations in temperature, pH, nutrients, or waste are more gradually absorbed and processed by the system. This reduces the likelihood of sudden ammonia spikes or algae blooms. For example, an accidental overfeeding is much less likely to disrupt a 40-gallon tank than a 10 gallon one.

A larger organic aquarium will also be able to function as a community tank, with multiple species living together in balance. Bigger tanks offer more ecological headroom, making it easier to support a variety of fish, shrimp, and snails without disrupting stability.

They take longer to mature, but once established, they can run with relatively little intervention. Plant maintenance tends to be less frequent, as space slows crowding. This makes them well suited to aquarists who want to step back, observe broader ecological patterns, and enjoy a more hands-off, big-picture rhythm.

CHOOSING THE RIGHT SHAPE

A tank's shape affects its habitat. Just as shallow wetlands and deep pools support different ecologies, your aquarium's proportions shape how light penetrates, how gases are exchanged, how nutrients move, and how your fish experience their world.

LIGHT

In long, shallow tanks, light is distributed more evenly through the water column, allowing plants throughout the system to photosynthesise efficiently. This supports consistent ammonia uptake, oxygen production, and water clarity across the tank. Tall, deep tanks, while visually striking, tend to cast the lower zones into shade – limiting plant activity and reducing their contribution to filtration.

GAS EXCHANGE

A broader water surface allows more efficient diffusion of oxygen into the tank and carbon dioxide out of it. Whilst we want to avoid losing too much carbon dioxide through gas exchange, narrow tanks with a smaller water surface area can cause it to accumulate to a dangerous level. This leads to a decrease in oxygen that will stress livestock if not managed.

WATER MOVEMENT

In a shallow, long tank, gentle horizontal flow patterns tend to distribute nutrients, oxygen, and waste evenly, supporting microbial and plant activity throughout. In a narrow deep tank, movement is unevenly distributed, leaving some regions untouched unless circulation is deliberately redirected.

ANIMAL BEHAVIOUR

Many of the small schooling fish best suited to organic aquariums (e.g. danios, rasboras, and white clouds) thrive in horizontal space. Fish interpret their surroundings by swimming room, not volume. A longer footprint allows for more natural movement, social interaction, and healthy territorial behaviour, even in relatively modest volumes.

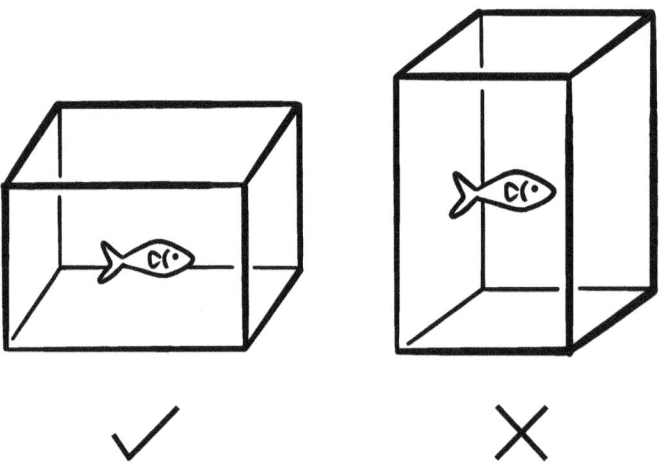

Altogether, tanks with more width than height provide the best support for plant health, water stability, and fish welfare in an organic system. They offer better light access and more surface area for gas exchange, and encourage steady, natural flow.

A note on open-top tanks

Most organic aquariums are kept open-topped. This setup allows more light to reach the water and makes it easy to access the tank for quick maintenance tasks. More importantly, it gives floating and emergent plants direct access to atmospheric carbon dioxide (we'll explore this more in the Plants chapter).

Open tanks do come with trade-offs. You'll need to regularly top up the water to compensate for evaporation, and certain fish species (especially those prone to jumping) are not suitable[13]. Still, for an organic setup focused on plant growth and natural ecological processes, these compromises are worth it.

HOW TO DECIDE

There is no universally 'correct' tank size or shape, only the setup that best suits your goals and the method's constraints.

If you enjoy tinkering and hands-on learning, nano tanks are compact, affordable, and give fast feedback. A 5–10 gallon setup would be the perfect responsive environment for you to learn in. If space is limited, but you want stability, a 20 gallon offers a great balance. If you want a resilient, slowly evolving ecosystem, large tanks offer stability, less frequent maintenance, and a more forgiving environment. A 40-gallon setup can provide a deeply rewarding space to observe and enjoy a maturing ecosystem. When choosing between two tanks of similar volume, opt for the one with a broader, shallower layout.

If you're curious and eager to learn through experimentation, consider starting with two small tanks rather than one large one. It is an affordable and revealing way to deepen your understanding. You will quickly learn how different soils, caps, plants, or animals affect an ecosystem when you can compare them side-by-side. And if (when) you fall in love with the hobby, plants from a small tank can be propagated to start a larger one, reducing costs.

Lastly, if you're unsure where to start, start small. Mistakes are part of learning, and it's far less stressful (and less expensive) to restart a 5-gallon shrimp tank than a 50-gallon community tank.

HOW DO I LIGHT MY AQUARIUM?

We light the system to match the pace of photosynthesis with the natural availability of carbon dioxide and nutrients. When plants grow in sync with what the system can provide, the tank stays balanced.

This distinction is important. In high-tech aquariums, strong lighting is paired with injected carbon dioxide and synthetic fertilisers to push fast, dense growth. In an organic aquarium, we take a slower approach: moderate lighting is calibrated to the system's natural rhythms, specifically, the slow release of carbon dioxide from soil and decomposition.

This principle is known as Liebig's Law of the Minimum: plant growth is limited by the scarcest resource in the system. In most organic aquariums, that limiting factor is carbon dioxide. No matter how intense your lighting is, plants can only grow as fast as the available carbon dioxide allows. When there is too much light and not enough carbon, the excess energy is left unused – creating ideal conditions for algae to take over.

CHOOSING A LIGHT FOR YOUR AQUARIUM

As we do not need fast, dense growth, specialist aquarium lighting is not required. A simple adjustable desk lamp – also known as an anglepoise or architect lamp – works perfectly for an organic setup. Affordable models like the IKEA Tertial accept standard bulbs and the adjustable arm makes it easy to experiment with lighting height and intensity[14]. If your aquarium is longer than 50 cm you will need more than one lamp. Alternatively, there are plenty of good quality, affordable LED aquarium lights on the market. Though try to find one with an adjustable mount so you can control the height of the light source. The takeaway here is that you don't need to purchase a high-end aquarium light to grow healthy plants.

For bulbs, start with a 6500K 'daylight' compact fluorescent (CFL) in the 15–23-watt range. These offer excellent light quality for plant growth while remaining energy efficient and inexpensive.

Start with the lamp positioned between 15–20 cm above the top of the tank. Observe for a week or two. If plants appear pale or stretched, lower the lamp slightly. If algae develops or leaves begin to brown, raise it a little. This responsive, observational approach suits the slower rhythms of organic aquariums and helps keep plant growth in balance with nutrient and carbon dioxide availability.

Some aquarists also experiment with natural sunlight instead of a lamp, placing their tanks near a window. While sunlight provides free, full-spectrum light, it can be difficult to control. Its intensity varies throughout the day and across seasons, which may lead to overheating, algae blooms, or erratic plant growth – especially in small tanks. For systems that are experimental in nature, this can be a workable option provided the aquarium can be easily moved or veiled from light. This gives you some control over light exposure and allows you to respond if sunlight becomes too strong. For most aquarists, however, artificial lighting remains the more predictable and manageable choice, offering consistent results with fewer variables to troubleshoot.

LIGHT DURATION

If given extended periods to photosynthesise (e.g. 12 hours of constant light), plants in an organic aquarium will deplete the available carbon dioxide. With time, this slows growth and creates an imbalance between light and carbon availability, giving algae an opportunity.

To prevent this, we use a siesta schedule. This split lighting method builds in a midday pause, allowing carbon dioxide levels to replenish naturally. While plants pause photosynthesis during the break, microbes continue producing carbon dioxide through decomposition[15]. When the lights come back on, plants start photosynthesising again and have more fuel for growth.

Importantly, this schedule disrupts algae. Unlike plants, algae require long, uninterrupted exposure to light to thrive. By breaking the lighting period in two, we limit algae's ability to photosynthesise, effectively giving plants the advantage[16].

Use a basic plug-in timer to implement this schedule:

- 4 hours of light in the morning
- 4-hour break (lights off)
- 4 more hours of light in the afternoon.

These lighting periods can then be adjusted based on how the ecosystem responds. Slow plant growth? Try 5:4:5. More algae appears? Try 4:5:4.

HOW DO I KEEP THE WATER MOVING?

An undersized internal filter (find the filter suited to your tank volume then get the size below it) or a small submersible water pump with adjustable flow is important for tanks larger than 20 gallons. Position the outlet below the water line to create slow, even movement without excessively disturbing plants or the water's surface.

To reduce maintenance and avoid redundancy, remove any media designed to trap small particles from your filter. These clog quickly and require frequent cleaning. By removing them, you allow the aquarium's decentralised filter (the plants, soil, and detritus crew) to do the work without interference. Keep the coarser filter media in to prevent waste from damaging the motor.

It's also worth considering what kind of microbial activity your filter encourages. Filters packed with high-surface-area media are designed to support nitrifying bacteria. While this is ideal in a conventional aquarium,

Equipment

in an organic system we want ammonia to remain available to plants. When nitrifying bacteria dominate, they convert ammonia into nitrate before plants can access it. This forces plants to work inefficiently, converting nitrate back into ammonia before they use it[17].

In tanks under 20 gallons, especially those that are densely planted and lightly stocked (e.g. shrimp jars), mechanical circulation is not necessary. In these systems, animal life and natural convection currents can provide enough movement to distribute nutrients and oxygen throughout the water column. However, passive systems require close observation. If detritus accumulates, or if plant growth slows, you may need to gently stir the water or perform more frequent water changes to prevent stagnation. A no-filter approach can work beautifully in small, balanced systems, but it depends on consistent care and careful observation.

DO I NEED TO HEAT IT?

If the room your aquarium is in holds a steady temperature, within the tolerance range of your fish and plants, then your system does not require a heater. However, if you plan to keep tropical species that require warmer conditions, and your room drops below that range at night or seasonally, a heater becomes essential.

Match your temperature to your fish and plant choices, and ensure it stays stable. A system that holds steadily at 24°C is healthier than one that swings between 20°C and 28°C – even if both fall within the general tolerance range of your fish and plants.

Cold stress can reduce microbial activity and weaken fish immunity. In water under 20°C plants can become dormant, meaning they stop producing new growth, halting the active removal of ammonia from the water. When these functions decline, your ecosystem becomes vulnerable.

Tanks under 20 gallons are particularly susceptible to temperature swings. Their low water volume changes temperature rapidly. In these setups, even hardy temperate species benefit from gentle heating to avoid disruptive fluctuations.

If you need to use a heater, preset models matched to your aquarium size are often sufficient. They are cost effective, easily sourced, and user friendly. By holding a consistent temperature, they maintain a steady environment for all the living components of your system.

In addition to heating your aquarium, you must be able to reliably monitor the temperature. A good-quality, glass thermometer placed inside the aquarium is an essential piece of equipment.

CAN I DECORATE IT WITH ROCKS OR DRIFTWOOD... OR A DINOSAUR SKULL?

Rocks, driftwood, and decorative items are all part of your hardscape. When used thoughtfully, it creates depth, texture, and structure while supporting plant growth, water flow, and animal behaviour.

But decorate in moderation: every piece of hardscape takes up space that could be used by plants, and some materials can alter your water chemistry.

CHEMICAL CONSIDERATIONS

We will explore water chemistry in more depth in the next chapter, but for the time being it is important to note that hardscape can affect your water.

Some rocks, like Seiryu stone, release minerals that raise water hardness. This is helpful if you have soft tap water but use sparingly. Once built into your aquascape, hardscape is difficult to remove, and excess mineral release will shift parameters too far over time.

Driftwood, on the other hand, can soften water and make it more acidic (lower its pH). Microbes also colonise the surface area of the submerged wood, but not always in a way that helps your system. The fungi and bacteria that grow on submerged driftwood consume nutrients from the water column. This reduces nutrient availability to plants, which slows their growth and can tip the system out of balance.

Equipment

When adding hardscape to an organic aquarium, less is more. A modest piece provides shelter and interest without tipping the system out of balance.

STRUCTURAL CONSIDERATIONS

Before adding driftwood, soak it for several days to remove excess tannins (compounds in the wood that make your aquarium tea-coloured) and help it sink. If it still floats or feels unstable, glue it to a rock to weigh it down.

If you are using very large, heavy, or angular pieces of rock, there is the risk that a pressure point could break the glass. To mitigate this risk, cut a piece of egg crate diffuser (a plastic grid structure) and position the rock on that. Do this before adding the substrate to your aquarium. This will distribute the weight of the rock over a larger surface area and prevent any point loads on the glass bottom. Add all other types of hardscape after the substrate is in place.

Once your hardscape is in place, gently tap each piece. If anything wobbles, secure it to a smaller rock using aquarium-safe superglue (cyanoacrylate gel is aquarium safe). A small piece of scrunched tissue between elements can increase surface area and help the glue bond more securely. Unstable hardscape can fall and break aquarium glass, so make sure everything is firmly in place.

RECOMMENDED HARDSCAPE MATERIALS

For your first aquarium, it is best to buy from reputable aquarium suppliers. This reduces the risk of introducing contaminants and pests. Always rinse your hardscape thoroughly before placing it in your tank.

Lava rock is especially useful as it easily broken into smaller pieces. If you're breaking rock apart, wrap it in a towel first, place it on a firm surface, wear eye protection, and strike carefully with a hammer. This controls flying fragments and keeps the process safe.

And yes, you can absolutely add a dinosaur skull. This is your aquarium. If you want a treasure chest, a shipwreck, or a miniature castle, include it.

There's nothing wrong with it if it makes you smile. Just make sure any decorative items are labelled as aquarium safe.

For rocks and driftwood, here are some common options to start you off:

ROCKS

- **Seiryu Stone:** Textured and mineral rich. Raises hardness. Use sparingly.
- **Dragon Stone (Ohko Stone):** Lightweight, earthy, and great for detail work.
- **Lava Rock:** Porous and versatile. Easy to break into smaller pieces.
- **River Stone:** Smooth and neutral. Good for base structure or accents.

WOOD

- **Manzanita Wood:** Hard, smooth, and low in tannins. Stable and ideal for plant attachment.
- **Spider Wood:** Branchy and striking.
- **Red Moor Wood:** Sculptural and lightweight.
- **Mopani Wood:** Dense and dark. Releases significant tannins.

Equipment

WHAT DO I NEED TO KEEP MY AQUARIUM CLEAN?

Maintenance can be divided into three simple tasks: plant pruning, cleaning the glass, and changing the water.

PLANT PRUNING

Pruning prevents overcrowding and helps control nutrient levels. As plants absorb nutrients from the water, trimming and removing surplus growth exports spent nutrients from the system, and encourages new growth.

A pair of long aquascaping scissors with a curved tip are helpful for pruning densely planted or small tanks, where precision is important. As you delve deeper into the hobby, a pair of aquascaping tweezers can make propagating cut stems and planting in tight spaces much easier. When building your first aquarium, however, you can simply plant by hand or with a pair of chopsticks (metal works best as there is less friction when you withdraw after planting). A small net is also useful for removing debris from the water's surface.

Prune every 2–4 weeks, depending on how quickly your plants grow. Trim back dying leaves and thin out areas that are becoming too dense. This helps with water flow and light penetration, and prevents too much detritus from accumulating at once.

If you don't wish to propagate your cut stems, you can offer them to local hobbyists through online aquarium groups or donate them to a local fish shop (sometimes in exchange for shop credit). Otherwise, remove the cuttings from your tank and set them aside to dry (at least 24 hours), then seal them in a bag before throwing them away. This prevents the accidental release of potentially invasive species into local waterways. When you keep an aquarium, you must be responsible for the nature within it, and protect the nature beyond it.

CLEANING THE GLASS

Algae or biofilm buildup on the aquarium glass is normal and easy to manage. Your clean-up crew will reduce the maintenance needed. Snails are excellent workers when it comes to removing algae and biofilm from surfaces. They graze throughout the day, keeping glass, hardscape, and plant leaves clean, and contribute to the detritus food web by shredding and cycling organic waste.

To clean the stubborn areas that your clean-up crew is ignoring, gently scrape the inside of the tank using a plastic card, or a razor blade scraper (only for glass tanks, and always with care). A new toothbrush can be used to clean hard-to-reach spots and to scrub hardscape. Never use household cleaning tools or soaps, as these can introduce harmful contaminants.

WATER CHANGES

Organic aquariums require fewer water changes than conventional setups, but they are still needed to replenish minerals and remove built-up waste products like nitrate.

In nature, aquatic ecosystems are constantly refreshed by rainfall, springs, and groundwater. These sources provide a steady supply of new water that helps maintain balance[18]. In your closed system, replacing evaporated water and the occasional water change serve the same role.

You'll need a clean bucket used only for aquarium tasks and a length of plastic tubing to siphon water out gently. In a stable system, a weekly top up to account for evaporation and a 10–25% water change every 3–6 months is usually enough. Larger water changes are needed if your water parameters swing out of a healthy range. Aquariums under 20 gallons or without water circulation can benefit from more frequent water changes. Always dechlorinate your tap water (more on this in the next chapter) and use your aquarium thermometer to match the temperature of the new water to the water in your tank.

Equipment

WHERE DO I GET EVERYTHING FROM?

There are many ways to source equipment, plants, and animals for your aquarium. Your choice will depend on your budget, location, and whether you're looking for new gear or open to second-hand finds. Here's where to start:

LOCAL AQUARIUM SHOPS AND GARDEN CENTRES

Independent aquarium shops and pet shops are a reliable place to buy nearly everything required for an organic aquarium. Garden centres are the best place to source the soil and the cap for your substrate. While prices may be slightly higher than online alternatives, the ability to ask questions and see equipment before purchase can be worth the cost, especially when starting out.

The benefit of purchasing plants from your local aquarium shop is that you can inspect them in person and ask questions about care. Look for tanks with good lighting, healthy leaves, and minimal algae. Prices may be higher than hobbyist sources, but the ability to hand-pick healthy plants is worth it.

When choosing fish, sourcing healthy animals from trusted sources will prevent a lot of issues later. While experienced aquarists often use a separate quarantine tank to isolate new arrivals, this isn't always practical for beginners. If you only have one tank, your best safeguard is choosing a local shop that already quarantines and treats its fish for common diseases before sale. Look for clear water, active fish, and employees who can answer questions about care, compatibility, and water conditions.

Be cautious of chain pet shops. Whilst there are some first-rate locations out there, you will typically find more knowledgeable – and passionate – staff in an independent shop.

ONLINE AQUARIUM SHOPS

Many online aquarium retailers offer a wider range of equipment, plants, and animals than physical shops, with the added convenience of online shopping. They're a great option if you want access to species not available locally. Make sure to choose retailers with good customer reviews, clear shipping policies, and a reputation for healthy, well-packaged plants and animals.

ONLINE MARKETPLACES

Amazon is a useful source for simple, affordable gear like thermometers, buckets, adjustable desk lamps, and power strips. While prices are competitive, quality can vary so always look for verified reviews, choose well-rated products, and avoid overly cheap items with no safety certifications.

Websites like eBay, Gumtree, and Facebook Marketplace often list second-hand tanks, lights, or full aquarium setups at a discount (and even for free). This can be a great way to build your system on a budget. Just be sure to inspect items carefully. Avoid tanks with deep scratches or warped frames, and if possible, request proof that the tank is watertight.

Many hobbyists often list plant bundles too. These can be excellent value, especially for fast-growing species like stem plants or floating plants. However, since you won't be seeing the plants in person, it's important to be cautious. Ask the seller for a recent photo of the actual plants you'll be receiving, not just a stock image. This gives you a better sense of the size, health, and cleanliness of what you're buying.

LOCAL HOBBYIST GROUPS

Aquarium clubs and local online groups (on platforms like Facebook or Reddit) are fantastic places to ask for recommendations, source second-hand gear, or borrow tools. Many aquarists generously share plant cuttings and fry from prolific breeders like endlers, cherry shrimp, and snails. This

Equipment

is easily the most cost-effective way to build your tank.

If you are sourcing animals from a local aquarist, be sure to ask questions about how the animals were kept and request a photo of the aquarium they are coming from. If a supplier is vague or evasive, it's best to look elsewhere.

3

Water

CAN I USE TAP WATER?

Tap water is the most common source of aquarium water. It contains a varied mix of dissolved minerals, metals, and chemical additives, which depend on your local water source, treatment process, and household plumbing. These elements influence how suitable your water is for aquatic life.

Chlorine or chloramine are added to tap water to make it safe to drink. While effective at killing harmful pathogens, these chemicals are dangerous to fish and microbes. Always treat your tap water before adding it to your aquarium. Even trace amounts of chlorine or chloramine can disrupt the ecosystem you're trying to establish.

Do not use a water conditioner that advertises multiple additional features as these can remove useful nutrients from the water[19]. Instead, use a simple conditioner that just dechlorinates.

HOW DO I TEST THE WATER?

As water travels through pipes and fixtures, it can pick up additional substances and change in composition (especially in older buildings). Test kits allow you to understand your water and track how your aquarium is progressing. Testing your water regularly is the best way to stay ahead of issues, especially once you have stocked your aquarium. For reliable results, invest in a liquid test kit that tests ammonia, nitrite, nitrate, pH, and hardness (GH/KH). The API® Freshwater Master Test Kit is the industry standard and is available through most aquarium retailers.

AMMONIA, NITRITE, AND NITRATE

In an organic aquarium, testing for ammonia, nitrite, and nitrate (measured in parts per million, or ppm) helps you understand whether your system has reached a healthy balance between waste production and plant intake. Ammonia and nitrite are toxic to aquatic life, even in small amounts, and should always remain at zero. The presence of either suggests that the system is under strain, either because there aren't yet enough plants to absorb available nutrients, or because something is overloading the system. This might happen in the early stages of setup, if there's excess detritus, or if a cap is too shallow and releasing soil into the water column. Low, steady levels of nitrate are not uncommon and can be used to gauge whether your plant mass is keeping up with nutrient input.

Regular testing lets you catch these imbalances early and adjust before they affect the health of your fish, plants, or microbial community. If ammonia or nitrite is detected, or if nitrate levels are creeping too high, perform a 25–50% water change to protect your animals and restore balance.

PH

The pH (potential of hydrogen) of water measures its acidity or alkalinity on a scale from 0 to 14. A pH of 7 is neutral, values below 7 are acidic, and values above 7 are alkaline (or basic). Most freshwater fish are comfortable in water with a pH between 6.5 and 7.5, though individual species have specific preferences. Sudden or extreme changes in pH can stress fish and damage biological processes. Maintaining a stable pH within the tolerable range of your plants and animals is more important than achieving an ideal number.

GH AND KH

Water hardness describes the concentration of certain minerals in your aquarium, and it comes in two forms: general hardness (GH) and carbonate hardness (KH). These are measured in ppm or degrees of hardness (dGH and dKH). Some plant and animal species prefer soft water, while others require hard water to thrive.

General hardness refers to the levels of dissolved calcium and magnesium in the water. These are valuable minerals: they support bone development in fish, are a source of nutrients for plants, and are critical for healthy shell and exoskeleton formation in snails and shrimp.

Carbonate hardness refers to the concentration of carbonates and bicarbonates in the water. KH indicates the buffering capacity of the water, meaning its ability to resist changes in pH. Carbonate and bicarbonate ions act like a cushion against changes in acidity. When acids enter the water, these ions neutralise them, helping to keep the pH stable. A higher KH value stabilises pH, while a very low KH can result in sudden and potentially harmful pH fluctuations.

In an organic aquarium, moderately hard water (8–12 dGH) is good. Soft water lacks essential minerals needed for healthy plant growth[20]. Fortunately, most tap water is moderately hard, but if yours is soft, its hardness can be increased.

For a built-in solution, you can add a small amount of Seiryu stone to your aquarium. This leaches carbonates and minerals over time. However, use it in moderation; too much can raise hardness excessively, and it's difficult to remove once integrated into the layout. A more flexible solution is to place crushed coral or oyster shells in a mesh bag inside a filter or near its outflow. These will also gradually raise general and carbonate hardness, whilst giving you the control to easily add or remove them as needed.

If there is a sudden KH drop or change in pH, you can add baking soda (3 grams per 10 gallons) to temporarily boost KH. Please note that this is a short-term fix only and should be used to stabilise the system while you find a long-term solution.

Avoid sulphate-based products like Epsom salts in an organic aquarium. In systems with accumulated detritus, excess sulphates can be converted by anaerobic bacteria into hydrogen sulphide, a toxic gas that harms plants and animals.

PH, KH, AND CARBON DIOXIDE

The relationship between pH, KH, and carbon dioxide is one of the main balancing acts in aquarium water chemistry. When carbon dioxide dissolves in water, it forms a weak acid called carbonic acid. This acidifies the water, lowering the pH. Carbonate hardness acts as a buffer. The carbonates react with the acid to form bicarbonates, preventing the pH from dropping too fast or too far. If KH is low (meaning there are fewer available carbonates), even small changes in carbon dioxide can cause big swings in pH.

Just as adding carbon dioxide lowers the pH, removing carbon dioxide causes the pH to rise. This happens throughout the day, when plants are photosynthesising and using up the available carbon dioxide, or when surface agitation (from an air stone or a hang-on filter) drives carbon dioxide out of the water. With less carbon dioxide in the water, there is less carbonic acid, so the pH goes up.

For example, if you have soft tap water with low KH and lots of plants, you might notice your pH reading 6.4 in the morning, but 7.6 in the evening. That's because your plants have depleted the carbon dioxide during the day, causing pH to rise.

These daily changes are called pH swings, and they can stress fish if they're too extreme. That's why it's important to keep a steady balance between pH, KH, and carbon dioxide. The goal is to have enough KH and carbon dioxide to maintain a stable pH (less than a one degree change) from day to night, helping fish and plants stay healthy and stress-free.

KH also affects the form of carbon available to plants. At higher KH and pH levels, carbon is more likely to exist as bicarbonate or carbonate ions rather than as dissolved carbon dioxide. Most aquatic plants can only use carbon dioxide directly, so when KH is too high, plant growth may slow. Finding the right KH level is a balancing act: high enough to stabilise pH, but not so high that it restricts access to carbon. However, some hardwater-adapted plant species (e.g. vallisneria and hornwort) can break bicarbonates and use them as an alternative carbon source.

Including bicarbonate-using species can increase the system's resilience. As a rule of thumb, plants that can tolerate very hard water can use bicarbonates. Specific species have been flagged in the plant field guide at the end of this book for easy reference.

To find the right balance, aim for a KH from 3–9dKH. This provides enough of a buffer to keep pH stable without significantly reducing carbon availability. Watch for signs: if your pH changes more than one degree across the day, or your plants appear stunted or yellow despite good lighting, you may need to adjust. You can gently raise KH using the methods outlined in the previous section. If KH is too high, use distilled water or rainwater during water changes to gradually dilute the hardness.

TDS

As you start exploring aquariums, you may come across the term TDS (total dissolved solids). This is a general measure of everything dissolved in your water: minerals, nutrients, salts, waste byproducts, the lot.

So why do some aquarists track it? TDS helps you spot trends. If your TDS is steadily rising, waste is likely building up or your plants aren't absorbing nutrients fast enough. A sudden drop could suggest a major change in water chemistry, like after a big water change or equipment issue. TDS doesn't tell you what is in the water, only how much, so it's best used as a broad health indicator rather than a precise tool.

That said, you don't need to worry about TDS when you're just starting out. In this approach, plant density manages TDS naturally by absorbing many of the nutrients and waste compounds that contribute to it. Focus on the basics first: ammonia, nitrite, nitrate, pH, and hardness (GH/KH). These have a more direct impact on fish and plant health.

This might sound like a lot to manage, but a healthy aquarium is not the result of perfect parameters. Instead of micromanaging each parameter, focus on creating conditions where balance can emerge on its own. In practice, it's simpler – and more forgiving – than it first appears.

4

Substrate

WHAT KIND OF SOIL CAN I USE?

Soil is a mixture of mineral particles, organic matter, water, air, and living organisms. The proportion of these components varies depending on the soil used. When choosing a soil for an organic aquarium, the main decision is whether to use potting soil or topsoil.

NUTRIENT-RICH POTTING SOIL

Potting soils are widely available and designed to support terrestrial plant growth in containers. They have a high percentage of organic matter – up to 50% – including ingredients like peat moss, coco coir, composted bark, and humus (a nutrient-rich substance that forms in soil after organics are decomposed, not to be confused with the Levantine dip). Its rich organic content fuels fast root development and vibrant plant growth, which is rewarding early on. Yet, the higher nutrient content often causes initial ammonia spikes, cloudy water, and algae blooms, especially if the tank is not densely planted. This can be disconcerting when you are new to the hobby.

Potting soil must be chosen with care. These soils vary widely in ingredients, making it harder to ensure you're getting an appropriate, aquarium-friendly mix. Avoid anything that includes added fertilisers, water-retaining crystals, or synthetic wetting agents. Check the label for an NPK value (Nitrogen-Phosphorus-Potassium) and look for very low values – ideally below 0.10:0.05:0.05[21]. Products labelled as 'organic' are more likely to be free of synthetic additives, but you should still read the ingredients list carefully.

Another common issue with potting soil is the presence of perlite or vermiculite. These lightweight particles improve drainage in pots but float when submerged, creating a messy layer on your tank's surface. While not harmful, they can be visually unappealing and difficult to remove once dispersed.

MINERAL-RICH TOPSOIL

Topsoil is lower in decomposing organics but rich in clay and minerals, which makes it good for steady, long-term plant health. As it has less organic material, it is less likely to cause initial algae blooms or ammonia spikes, making it the safer option when starting out.

Not all topsoil is created equal, and a little observation goes a long way towards choosing a soil that will support healthy aquarium life.

If sourcing soil from a garden centre, choose a product labelled simply as organic topsoil. Be cautious of soils labelled as 'garden soil' or 'raised bed mix,' as these often contain added fertilisers, compost, or wetting agents.

If collecting soil from your own garden, look for undisturbed areas away from roads and treated lawns. Dig below the surface – about 5–10 cm down – to access soil that hasn't been exposed to any recent potential contamination.

Use your senses to identify promising soil: good soil should feel loamy, holding its shape when gently squeezed but crumbling apart with light pressure. It should smell earthy and rich, like a forest floor. If it smells sour, vinegary, or like rotten eggs, avoid it. These odours suggest excess anaerobic decomposition, which can introduce toxins and disrupt your aquarium's balance. Look for dark brown or black soil with a mix of fine particles and small decomposed plant matter. Avoid grey, pale, or heavily compacted soil.

The location where you dig influences the microbial composition of the soil. As a rough guide, soil from an area with fast-growing plants (like vegetable beds or grassy patches) is more likely to be rich in bacteria, which are the microbes most active in early decomposition and nutrient cycling. As explained by Lowenfels, these areas tend to support a bacterially dominated soil ecosystem, which mirrors the kind of microbial activity we want to encourage in our organic aquarium[22]. Avoid soil from shady, slow-growing spots like under trees or in dense brush, as these will be fungally dominated and decompose less predictably once submerged.

Only use soil from your own garden if you know it is free of contaminants. If in doubt, it is better to purchase a bag of topsoil.

OTHER OPTIONS

Some aquarists have had success using bagged pond soil, typically available at aquatic nurseries for planting in outdoor ponds. These products are generally composed of a dense mixture of clay, silt, and fine mineral particles, with minimal added organic matter. Because they are designed for submerged conditions, pond soils are less likely to cloud the water or leach excessive nutrients. Their composition naturally supports the development of an anaerobic-to-aerobic gradient that benefits aquatic plant roots and microbial communities. Though pond soil is harder to source, it is a great option.

In contrast, aquarium-specific plant substrates (the bags of small black balls you find in aquarium shops) are engineered for high-tech aquarium setups that rely on carbon dioxide injection and routine dosing with synthetic fertilisers. While these substrates can support robust plant growth in those systems, they are not suited to organic aquariums. These products do not have enough organic matter needed for decomposition, and they do not provide the microbial habitat required to sustain a low-tech, soil-based ecosystem. For anyone creating an organic aquarium, these products offer the wrong kind of support at a significantly higher cost.

HOW DO I PREPARE THE SOIL?

Once you've chosen your soil, the next step is to prepare it for your aquarium.

Start by spreading your soil out in a shallow tray, container, or even in the tank itself. Remove any stones or plant matter thicker than a pencil (e.g. sticks, large roots, rocks, or bark chunks). Removing these larger components will make layering easier and reduce the risk of plant matter floating up. Do not sift the soil. If it is reduced to a fine powder, you lower the number of organics available for decomposition and increase the risk of soil compaction due to its finer structure.

If your soil's structure is naturally fine and you are worried about compaction, mix the soil with inert gravel (5–10 mm diameter): approximately 1 part gravel to 3 parts soil will vary the soil's structure and ensure roots and water can still penetrate the soil layer.

Once again, trust your senses. Does the soil smell fresh and earthy, or is there a sour, chemical, or rotten odour? Is the texture crumbly and loamy, or is it powdery, gritty, or full of large chunks? What colour do you see? Dark brown or black is usually a good sign. It's natural to feel eager to move forward, but taking a moment to assess the soil now can save you a lot of frustration later. It's much easier to pivot at this stage than to troubleshoot a fully planted tank. If you're unsure, don't hesitate to ask for help. Online aquarium communities can be a great resource – someone may have used the same brand of bagged soil or had similar questions. (You'll find a list of recommended forums at the back of this book.) A second opinion from an experienced hobbyist can offer peace of mind before you commit.

Do not sterilise or bake the soil. Doing so destroys the beneficial microbial communities that help establish a soil-based tank in the first place.

What about mineralising soil?

If you have been researching soil-based aquariums, you have likely come across mineralisation discussions. In simple terms, mineralisation is a soil preparation method that involves soaking and drying soil repeatedly over several weeks. The goal is to pre-decompose unstable organic material before the soil enters the aquarium[23].

The process typically involves:

- Soaking the soil in water for 1–2 days
- Draining and allowing it to dry completely
- Repeating the soak/dry cycle 3–4 times.

The science behind mineralisation is straightforward. Each wetting cycle activates decomposing bacteria that break down organic compounds. The drying phase then kills many of these bacteria, making their cellular contents available as nutrients while removing the more volatile organics. The result is a more stable substrate that releases nutrients gradually rather than in the initial surge of organics typical of fresh soils.

This method can reduce early ammonia spikes and create a cleaner startup, especially when using nutrient-rich potting soils. Mineralisation is effective but time-consuming, and not necessary for success. If you're working in a small space, short on time, or simply eager to get started, this step is optional.

WHAT DO I USE FOR THE CAP?

There are two main options for your cap material: coarse sand, or fine gravel.

Sand can be sourced from your local garden centre or pool equipment shop. Choose products labelled as play sand or pool filter sand (with a grade of 16/30 or coarser). These are safe and cost effective options to use in your aquarium. Do not use construction sand as this has not been through the same screening process and can introduce contaminants into your aquarium.

If you would prefer to use a fine gravel, it is recommended to source this from an aquarium shop. Most gravels available from garden centres are too large or sharp for aquarium use. For an organic aquarium, we want to ensure a consistent particle size with a rounded profile. This will help form the oxidised microzone and ensure any bottom-dwelling animals are not injured.

Sourcing cap material from an aquarium shop will have a higher price tag; however, the result can be worth the additional cost if you have a specific aesthetic in mind for your aquascape.

HOW DEEP SHOULD THE SUBSTRATE BE?

As explained earlier, an organic aquarium substrate is made up of two layers: a soil layer, and a cap layer. Each has a specific role, and getting the proportions right supports these roles.

SOIL LAYER

In most aquariums, a soil depth of 2.5 cm is ideal. For tanks under 10 gallons, 2 cm is sufficient. Larger tanks can accommodate a slightly deeper soil bed – up to 4 cm – especially around larger rooted plants.

Place less soil in areas where you plan to position hardscape. Soil placed under hardscape can compact and turn anaerobic, especially if out of reach from plant roots. This can create toxins and, in extreme cases, throw your system out of balance.

CAP LAYER

Cap depth should be scaled to match the particle size. As a rule of thumb, when using coarse sand (0.5–2 mm, about the size of granulated sugar) the cap depth should be 2.5 cm. When using fine gravel (2–3 mm, about the size of steel-cut oats) the cap depth should be 3.5–4 cm. Shallower than this will risk excess nutrients leaching into the water column. Do not use anything larger than pea gravel (5 mm, about the size of pepper corns), as it is too porous.

Substrate

Increase the depth of your cap if you see soil coming through, experience algae blooms, or have frequent ammonia spikes. Add in small increments of 0.5–1 cm until you have found a balance.

This allows for gentle water movement through the substrate while keeping the soil contained. To create an oxidised microzone, the cap must be breathable. A cap that is too fine or too deep can smother the soil, while one that is too coarse or too shallow risks not containing the soil below.

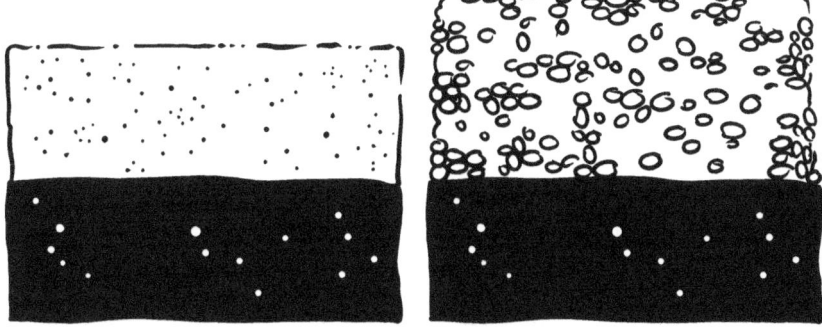

When adding these layers to your aquarium, you can estimate them. It does not have to be exact to the millimetre. However, it can be difficult to gauge the depth of the cap, especially in the central area of the aquarium. The easiest way to check your substrate depth is to transfer your desired soil and cap measurements onto a cocktail stick or coffee stirrer. You can then use it as a measure, checking depth against the marked lines by pushing it through the substrate.

HOW LONG WILL THE SOIL LAST?

Like any nutrient source, soil will not last forever – the carbon released through decomposition will eventually be depleted. Most substrates remain effective for around 2 to 3 years, though this depends on planting density, fish load, and water conditions[24].

You'll know the substrate carbon stores are running out when plant growth slows despite stable lighting and water parameters. Rooted plants may pale or stop producing new shoots. At that point, you can either begin routinely adding root tabs near heavy feeders or rebuild your aquarium with fresh soil.

Recognising this long-term cycle is all part of the ecosystem's natural progression.

WILL SOIL MAKE MY AQUARIUM WATER YELLOW?

It is natural for a soil-based aquarium to develop a slight yellow or tea-coloured tint. This comes from tannins in the soil and dissolved organic carbon released during decomposition. These compounds are beneficial to the ecosystem. The dissolved organic carbon binds to toxic metals and forms a protective coating on fish cells (especially their gills), helping buffer against acidity and trace pollutants[25]. This tint is a hallmark of healthy substrate activity, not a sign of poor water quality.

If you want clearer water, increase the frequency of your water changes or temporarily use activated carbon filtration (if you are using a filter). Otherwise, embrace the tint as a feature of your aquarium. It adds a striking natural aesthetic and brings out the colours of your fish beautifully.

If you're finding the idea of adding soil to your new aquarium a little daunting, don't worry – you're not alone. There's a lot to take in at first; you shouldn't expect to do everything perfectly right away. What matters more is learning to observe and to stay curious.

DISCLAIMER: Even with careful planning and perfect execution, your aquarium may surprise you – and not always in good ways! Your water might turn the colour of strong tea from tannins, plants may stubbornly refuse to grow, or algae might throw an unexpected party. This isn't a reflection of your skills or attention to detail – it is simply nature being out of our control. These frustrations often teach us more than our successes. When things don't work out as expected, embrace the learning opportunity, document what happened, and share your experience with the online communities listed at the back of this book. Fellow aquarists love troubleshooting together, and your story might help someone else facing similar challenges. Remember: every experienced aquarist has a story that starts with 'Well, it didn't go as planned...'

5

Plants

WHICH PLANTS SHOULD I GET?

An organic aquarium needs plants. Lots of them. It needs plants which can produce consistent, healthy growth in low light and with moderate levels of carbon dioxide. There are four categories of plant that every organic aquarium should have:

1. FLOATING PLANTS

Floating plants are typically small, fast-growing species such as duckweed, Amazon frogbit, red root floaters, and salvinia. They require no substrate and float freely on the water's surface, making them easy to manage in low-tech setups. In an organic aquarium, floating plants are essential. They absorb excess nutrients, provide shade that limits algae growth, offer shelter for fish and fry, and even slow the rate of evaporation.

What makes floating plants especially valuable is the 'aerial advantage'[26]. They live above and below the water. Floating plants absorb nutrients from the water column and tap into atmospheric carbon dioxide, which is hundreds of times more abundant than dissolved carbon dioxide underwater. Remember Liebig's Law of the Minimum? By accessing atmospheric carbon dioxide, their growth is not limited by the carbon dioxide produced through decomposition within the aquarium. As a result, they can grow rapidly, even in low-tech setups.

Their fast growth enables them to remove ammonia and other waste nutrients from the water more efficiently than submerged plants early in the tank's life. This helps prevent nutrient accumulation that could otherwise fuel algae blooms. Furthermore, floating plants create a pathway for atmospheric carbon to enter the system: carbon dioxide is drawn in through new growth, and older leaves release it into the system as they decompose. Aquatic systems with floating or emergent growth (some aquatic plants can grow up and out of the water) exhibit up to three times the biological activity of systems without them[27].

2. ROOT-FEEDING PLANTS

Root-feeding plants are typically rosette-forming species such as cryptocoryne, echinodorus, sagittaria, and vallisneria, which anchor deeply and draw nutrients primarily from the substrate.

As discussed in Objective 3, plants that develop extensive root systems oxygenate the substrate. The oxygen-rich areas surrounding plant roots host a thriving community of microbes, which in turn, unlock nutrients that would have otherwise been unavailable to the plant. With time, this partnership builds a biologically active substrate that nourishes plants and microbes.

3. WATER COLUMN FEEDERS

Water column feeders are typically fast-growing stem plants such as bacopa, rotala, hygrophila, and pearlweed, as well as free-floating species like hornwort, which absorb nutrients directly through their leaves rather than roots.

Fast-growing plants are essential during your aquarium's early stages. These plants rapidly absorb excess nutrients and ammonia from the water. This fast growth stabilises your aquarium environment and helps to prevent early algae blooms. They might dominate at

Plants

the beginning, but as your aquarium matures, they can be gradually replaced or pruned back to allow more space for slower-growing species.

4. EPIPHYTES AND MOSSES

Epiphytes are technically defined as plants that grow on other plants. In an aquarium, they are attached to hardscape via their rhizome: a thick, horizontal stem that anchors the plant and produces both roots and leaves. Be careful not to bury the rhizome in substrate, as doing so leads to rot and eventual plant death. Epiphytes grow slowly, but their steady presence offers long-term stability with minimal maintenance. Common examples include Java fern and anubias.

Mosses are small, non-vascular plants (meaning they lack the internal tubes that vascular plants use to transport water, nutrients, and sugars). Instead, they absorb moisture and nutrients directly across their entire surface. Unlike rooted plants, mosses don't need soil and are often used to cover hardscape or create natural-looking drapes and carpets in the aquarium. Popular aquarium mosses include Java moss and Christmas moss.

Epiphytes and mosses are attached to surfaces such as rocks, driftwood, or decorations and absorb nutrients directly from the water. They maximise planting space by thriving in areas where other plants can't grow.

At the end of this book, you will find a field guide with an overview of common plants in each of the above categories. It will help you navigate the decision-making process.

HOW MANY PLANTS SHOULD I GET?

Aim to cover at least 50% of the substrate (excluding hardscape) with plants at setup. In ecological terms, this is known as basal cover: the portion of the ground occupied by the base of the plant. It's different from foliar cover, which refers to how far the leaves or stems spread out above ground.

A tank with high basal cover will stabilise faster, outcompete algae, and provide better water quality. Sparse plantings leave excess nutrients in the water column and slow beneficial bacterial activity in the soil, which can trigger algae blooms and delay cycling.

To help visualise the required coverage, picture 5 cm squares covering the entire floor of your tank, like a chessboard. Now, block out any squares that are occupied by hardscape. From the remaining squares, half need to have at least one plant in them.

For example, a bushy rosette like echinodorus may have large leaves that stretch over multiple squares, but if its root base only sits in one, it only counts as one. What matters most is how much of the substrate is in contact with roots, not how leafy the plant looks from above.

This doesn't mean you need to go out and buy dozens of potted plants; you can easily divide one plant across multiple squares. Likewise, if you're on a budget and can't plant densely right away, that's okay. Many aquatic plants can be propagated by trimming and replanting healthy growth. Just be aware that this will delay how soon you can add fish – since low plant mass can lead to toxic ammonia levels – but waiting a few extra weeks can save money and still allow you to reach the critical plant mass needed for stability.

Some plants may not thrive immediately. It's normal for new additions (especially those grown out of water before sale) to 'melt': shedding old leaves as they adapt to submerged life. This doesn't mean the plant is dead. If melt occurs, trim the disintegrating leaves but leave the roots undisturbed; the plant will typically produce new growth once it has adjusted to its new environment. Be careful not to discard a plant which is still adapting.

When starting out, focus on function and variety rather than creating the perfect layout. Choose a mix of species that include at least one plant from each of the four categories.

DO I NEED TO FERTILISE MY PLANTS?

Plants need a mix of macronutrients (e.g. nitrogen, phosphorus, and potassium) and micronutrients (e.g. iron, boron, and zinc) to grow. As established earlier, all the essential plant nutrients are provided passively by the soil and actively each time you add fish food to your aquarium[28]. But even with your detrital crew cycling nutrients, there are two that may require your attention: one macronutrient, potassium (K), and one micronutrient, iron (Fe). These nutrients are often the first to be depleted in the water column and can halt plant growth.

Potassium is essential for healthy plant function. It helps regulate water balance in plant cells and supports overall growth. Unlike nitrogen or phosphorus, however, potassium is not sufficiently supplied through fish waste or decomposition. If your tap water and soil are both low in potassium, your plants may begin to show signs of deficiency. Symptoms of potassium deficiency include yellowing or browning along leaf edges, and tiny round holes in leaves (often called pinholes) which gradually widen and die back.

Iron is crucial for chlorophyll production, which keeps leaves green and supports photosynthesis. In an organic aquarium, iron is available to rooted plants through the soil, but it's absent from the water column. This causes problems for floating plants as they do not have access to the substrate iron. The classic symptom of iron deficiency is chlorosis: the yellowing of new leaves while older ones remain green. You may also notice slow growth or pale colouring in species that are normally vibrant.

The simplest and safest way to correct either of these deficiencies is to use an off-the-shelf liquid potassium and iron fertiliser. API® Leaf Zone is the perfect complement here as it contains just potassium and iron, with no nitrogen or phosphorus. This means it will support your plants without upsetting the balance of your ecosystem.

Only dose if symptoms appear (as they are not necessarily in every system) and dose lightly, starting at half strength. Observe and only increase if deficiencies persist. When you're just starting out, skip DIY mixes as finding the right dose can be difficult and unpredictable.

HOW ARE PLANTS SOLD?

Most aquarium plants are sold either as potted or in-vitro specimens. Both options have their place, but if you are on a tight budget, start by trying to source free local cuttings to build up your plant mass.

POTTED PLANTS

Potted plants are the most common option found in local aquarium shops and garden centres. The plant is usually rooted in rock wool, a sponge-like material that holds moisture. This must be removed entirely before planting, as it can trap debris and restrict root development. To free the plant, gently split apart the rock wool, then use a fork to remove any remaining material from the roots. Potted plants are typically more robust than in-vitro plants and allow you to inspect them for health before purchase. Be mindful that plants may carry unwanted snails, algae, or other hitchhikers. It's recommended to rinse them thoroughly in dechlorinated water and inspect each plant carefully before introducing them to your aquarium. If you're unsure, a short quarantine period in a separate container can help reduce the risk of introducing pests into your setup.

IN-VITRO PLANTS

In-vitro (tissue culture) plants are grown in sterile, sealed containers filled with nutrient gel. These high-quality plants are commonly sold through online retailers as they are easy to ship. They're a clean and controlled option, guaranteed free from snails, algae, and pesticides – ideal if you're starting a tank and want to avoid unwanted hitchhikers. Each cup usually contains several small plantlets that can be separated and spread around your aquarium. However, they are more expensive per plant and tend to be more prone to melt during the transition into a new environment. With proper care, most recover and adapt over time.

CUTTINGS

When sourcing from local hobbyists, it's common to receive a bundle of stem plant cuttings rather than potted, rooted plants. Don't worry if they don't have roots yet; most fast-growing species will grow them quickly once planted or even when left free-floating under good light. It's an affordable, effective way to fill out your tank. Just rinse and inspect them before planting.

HOW DO I KNOW IF I'M BUYING A HEALTHY PLANT?

Filling your aquarium with weak or dying plants will not create a healthy ecosystem. To give your aquarium the best chance of success, it's essential to start with strong, healthy specimens. Only growing plants can remove toxins from the water[29].

The clearest sign of a healthy plant is new growth[30]. Fresh leaves, new shoots, and branching roots all indicate that the plant is actively growing and has adjusted well to its environment. If you see signs of fresh, bright green or reddish tips, you're onto a winner.

CAN I GROW HOUSEPLANTS FROM MY AQUARIUM?

Many hobbyists enjoy experimenting with houseplant cuttings or even sprouting common herbs and vegetables at the edges of their tanks. These semi-aquatic additions add some novelty and actively support the water quality of your system.

Many common houseplants like pothos, peace lily, or spider plants will root happily in water and thrive in your open-top aquarium. Some aquarists even use the excess nutrients in the aquarium to sprout garlic, avocado seeds, and sweet potatoes. It's small-scale aquaponics, and while you won't be harvesting full meals anytime soon, it's a fun method to recycle nutrients and explore plant growth in new ways.

You don't need a complicated setup to position these plants. Start by removing all the potting soil from the plants' roots, then decide where to place them. The goal is to suspend the plants so that their roots access the water without submerging the plants themselves. If your hardscape extends above the waterline, you can use it as a structure to support your houseplants. Otherwise, you can use soft plant twist ties to hook your plants in place.

Alternatively, you can purchase hydroponic plant holders to hang on the edge of your aquarium. Brands such as Poth-O-Carry® create holders with specific species in mind, meaning they position your plant at its ideal height (and they often look tidier than DIY methods).

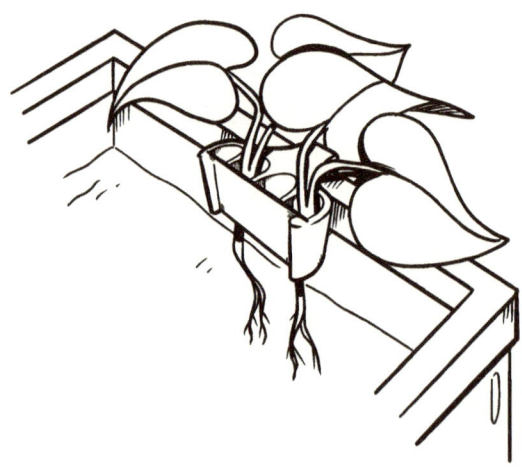

Plants

As covered earlier, plants that grow above the waterline have access to atmospheric carbon dioxide. This means they can grow quickly and absorb nutrients efficiently, helping to reduce the load on your in-tank plants. Their roots dangle into the aquarium, taking up nitrogen and nutrients much like floating plants do. In return, they release oxygen, stabilise the water, and offer a simple way to expand the system.

These projects are entirely optional, but they highlight something important: an aquarium doesn't have to end at the water's surface. In an organic system, every part of the tank, and even the space around it, can play a role in the larger cycle of growth, decay, and renewal. Whether you're trailing pothos or watching garlic sprout, these small additions can deepen your connection to the system you're building.

> **DISCLAIMER**: Research invasive species in your region before collecting, cultivating, or disposing of any aquatic plants. Never release plants, cuttings, trimmings, or aquarium waste into waterways, storm drains, or natural areas – even native species can become problematic when introduced to new locations. Dispose of excess plant material by thoroughly drying and bagging before disposal. If collecting plants, verify local regulations and obtain necessary permissions. By acting responsibly, your actions prevent ecological damage and protect aquatic ecosystems for future generations.

6

Animals

WHEN CAN I ADD FISH AND INVERTEBRATES?

An organic aquarium needs time to settle before animals can be safely introduced. Adding fish or invertebrates too early can overwhelm the system before it is ready. But that doesn't mean there's nothing to see in those first few weeks. One of the joys of this approach is observing the system stabilise, a principle known as ecological succession:

> Ecological succession is the process by which the mix of species and habitat in an area changes over time. Gradually, these communities replace one another until a 'climax community' – like a mature forest – is reached[31].

Though your aquarium is a closed system, it's still governed by the same biological principles that shape ponds, wetlands, and other aquatic ecosystems. In the first few months, different groups of organisms take turns establishing themselves, as the system moves towards balance. Understanding this natural sequence helps you know when to add animals, and when to wait. We can understand succession in an organic aquarium as unfolding in three stages:

STAGE 1: PIONEER SPECIES (WEEKS 0-4)

The early phase of any organic setup is dynamic and unpredictable. The soil is adjusting to being submerged, plants are adapting to their new environment, and the first pioneer species (bacteria, microfauna, and algae) begin to multiply. During this stage, you'll likely see copepods, ostracods, and detritus worms crawling through the substrate or clinging to the glass. These tiny organisms are part of the detritus food web, and their presence is an excellent sign that your system is beginning to take shape.

This stage is characterised by change. A white, cloudy tank during the first week is common, as bacteria multiply rapidly in response to nutrients leaching from the soil. This is a normal part of the equilibration process. Similarly, brown diatom algae may coat surfaces in the first few weeks. These early colonisers typically disappear on their own as plants establish dominance and nutrient competition increases. A thin, slippery biofilm may also appear on hardscape, glass, or plant leaves. This is not a problem. In later stages, your snails, shrimp, and some fish will graze on it, helping convert it into usable nutrients for the rest of the system.

It's important to be patient here. Even if tests show traces of ammonia or nitrite, it's best to avoid interfering. As plants grow and establish, they will naturally absorb these compounds. Frequent water changes can delay this process by altering the chemical environment that plants are trying to adapt to.

Whilst it is recommended to avoid intervening during this period, there is a situation where it is advised. If you've started with fewer plants and are relying on growth and propagation over time to reach the critical

plant mass, algae may begin to outcompete your plants. In this case, gentle interventions can help tip the balance back in favour of plant life. Reduce lighting to 4–6 hours per day (start by trying 3 hours on, 5 hours off, 3 hours on), and perform small water changes (10–25%) twice a week for the first 4 weeks. Scrape algae from the glass and remove hair algae manually. If algae are still outcompeting your plants, consider purchasing additional floating plants and fast-growing water-column feeders to absorb excess nutrients.

Do not use algaecides. These chemical shortcuts disrupt the delicate biological processes that your system is working to establish. With time, most algae blooms fade on their own as plant mass increases and the nutrient balance shifts. There will always be some algae in your aquarium; it is a natural and even beneficial part of your freshwater ecosystem – provided it doesn't take over.

Fish and invertebrates should not be added during this stage. Let the plants and microbes lead the way.

STAGE 2: INTERMEDIATE SPECIES (WEEKS 4–8)

Once your plants are growing steadily and your water tests show a stable pH and zero ammonia and nitrite, you can add your first animals: the

clean-up crew. Snails and shrimp are excellent early inhabitants. They're hardy, and they play a valuable role in grazing algae and breaking down detritus.

These invertebrates also serve as indicators. If they remain healthy and active, it's a good sign that your system is ready to support more complex life. And in many cases, this stage can be a satisfying endpoint. A planted aquarium with an active shrimp colony can be incredibly beautiful, lively, and easy to maintain.

There is no need to rush beyond this stage. Let the ecosystem continue to mature at its own pace.

STAGE 3: CLIMAX COMMUNITY (WEEK 8 ONWARDS)

It takes approximately 8 weeks for the chemistry of the submerged soil to stabilise[32]. If ammonia and nitrite remain at zero, your pH is steady, and plants are thriving, then the system may be ready to support fish. However, if you're still seeing ammonia or nitrite spikes, or experiencing regular pH swings, wait. The system is not ready. It's far better to wait a few more weeks than to spend every day worrying about your new fish as they struggle in a toxic environment. Fish should only be added once the tank shows consistent, stable water parameters and clear signs of balance.

Once your system is stable you can add fish. Begin slowly. Start with small, hardy species, and observe them closely. Test your water daily for 2 weeks after adding fish, watching for ammonia or nitrite spikes and monitoring fish behaviour. If everything remains stable (e.g. no toxins, no algae blooms, no signs of stress) you can gradually add more fish in small groups over time.

This staggered approach allows your plants and microbes to adjust to the increased bioload. Give the system time to respond to each new addition before introducing more.

FISH-IN VS. FISHLESS CYCLE

Some aquarists add fish to soil-based aquariums on day one. Soil bacteria act as a starter culture – like using an established aquarium's filter media – making traditional cycling unnecessary. However, an organic aquarium relies on many factors working together. As you learn about and build aquariums, mistakes are to be expected. For this reason, it's safer – and more humane – to wait before adding animals. Waiting gives your plants a head start, and lets you observe and adjust the ecosystem while lowering risks to your fish and invertebrates.

There's wisdom in the saying: 'good things happen slowly; bad things happen fast.' Embrace the gradual process, and you'll be rewarded with a stable, mature ecosystem that can keep itself in balance.

WHICH SPECIES CAN I KEEP?

An organic aquarium must be stocked with animals that match the natural rhythms and limits of the system. Focus on species that inherently suit the features of this approach. If they originate from low-flow, shaded, densely planted habitats they will likely thrive.

It is important to choose species that have a low bioload: the total amount of waste an organism contributes to the system. A low bioload ensures that the natural waste processing systems of your organic aquarium are not overloaded. If you have too high a bioload, you risk overwhelming your system, disrupting the balance you've achieved. For this reason, small species (often called nano fish) are ideal.

Species such as ember tetras, chili rasboras, celestial pearl danios, or white cloud mountain minnows stay under 4 cm, are peaceful, and thrive in groups. A school of 6–10 fish adds movement to the mid-water without generating excessive waste. They feel secure among plants and often display their best colours in a well-planted tank. As mentioned earlier, avoid fish known to jump (like hatchetfish or certain danios) if your aquarium is open topped.

Alternatively, you can choose a solitary 'centrepiece' fish; a honey gourami or a plakat betta (short-finned betta) are great options. Keep only one of these centrepiece fish per tank to avoid territorial aggression. These fish are relatively sedate and will often hover near plants or at the surface. They are visually striking and interesting to observe, especially when the males construct their floating bubble nests. Both species possess a labyrinth organ that allows them to breathe atmospheric air, so ensure they have access to the water's surface. Just note that these species will likely prey on baby shrimp.

And of course, an organic aquarium would be incomplete without its clean-up crew. Cherry shrimp (neocaridina) are excellent grazers, picking at biofilm and soft algae while helping to keep surfaces clean. Amano shrimp are larger and renowned for their appetite for algae, making them ideal tank helpers. Snails also play a vital role: nerite snails eat stubborn green algae (and cannot reproduce in freshwater, preventing population booms), while ramshorn snails consume decaying organics. Malaysian trumpet snails are especially useful in soil-based tanks; they burrow amongst the cap, mixing and aerating the accumulated detritus as they search for food. Avoid pond snails as these will eat healthy plant tissue; stick to species that only consume decaying organics. If your snail population begins to grow too quickly, reduce feeding slightly and numbers will stabilise with time. A well-chosen mix of shrimp and snails will support the detritus food web and reduce the need for intervention.

Finally, the clean-up crew isn't limited to invertebrates. Otocinclus catfish are a gentle, algae-grazing fish that are a perfect match for organic systems. A small group of otocinclus will tirelessly rasp biofilm and soft algae from plant leaves and glass, all the while contributing very little waste. Their peaceful nature and hard-working habits make them one of

Animals

the few algae-eating fish truly suited to low-tech planted tanks.

At the end of this book, you will find a field guide with an overview of common fish and invertebrates in the aquarium hobby. The curated selection is by no means exhaustive, but it does introduce species with proven success in organic setups.

HOW MANY SHOULD I ADD?

Stocking an organic aquarium, like everything else in an organic aquarium, is all about balance. Your tank has a natural limit, determined by how many nutrients your plants can absorb and how efficiently your detrital food web can process waste. As we are not outsourcing waste management to a powerful filter, you'll keep fewer animals than in a conventional setup.

Here's a rough guide to how many animals your tank can support, depending on its size:
- Under 7 gallons: snails and shrimp only. The limited water volume and plant mass make it difficult to support fish.
- 7–10 gallons: choose either a school of 6 nano fish or a single centrepiece fish, along with your clean-up crew of snails and shrimp.
- 10–20 gallons: offers more flexibility. You might keep a larger school of nano fish, or one peaceful centrepiece fish with a smaller school, alongside your clean-up crew.
- 20 gallons and larger: you can typically start with 8–12 fish, supported by your clean-up crew. If, after a few weeks, your plants are growing well, algae are minimal, and water tests consistently show zero ammonia, you can consider adding more stock gradually. Always watch your tank closely. Persistent cloudiness, rising nitrates, algae blooms, or signs of fish stress are all indicators that you've exceeded your system's capacity. **When in doubt, under-stock.** You can always add more fish later, but recovering from an overloaded tank is far more difficult.

There is no magic formula here. Start light, observe your tank, and let it guide you.

HOW DO I INTRODUCE MICROFAUNA?

As your new system stabilises, a variety of microfauna will begin to appear – seemingly from thin air. These pioneers are hitchhikers; inadvertently, though beneficially, introduced through your soil and plants. They are welcome residents, and their presence is a sign of a healthy ecosystem.

In addition to these hitchhikers, you may wish to actively introduce some larger members to your detrital crew. There are three ways to add microfauna: you can purchase them from a specialist supplier; you can source them from a fellow hobbyist; or you can culture your own wild specimens.

The easiest and most reliable option is to source microfauna from a specialist. There are a handful of shops that specialise in botanicals and microfauna cultures, and you can be confident that they are suitable to your aquarium. However, this is still an emerging area of the hobby so it may not be available in your region.

If you are unable to source from a supplier, you can appeal to local hobbyists through online groups or at your local aquarium shop. Whilst this request may garner some strange looks, it is a great way of introducing new species from a controlled environment. If you would prefer to culture your own wild microfauna, there are instructions in the How-to section of this book.

Whilst this method is rewarding, it is experimental by nature and does add some risk as you may inadvertently introduce parasitic microfauna or otherwise dangerous contaminants to your aquarium. It is also, sadly, unreasonable to assume that everyone has access to clean waterways. For those reasons, it is recommended to source from either a specialist or a local hobbyist.

PROTECTING MICROFAUNA WITH BOTANICALS

When you introduce fish, your microfauna population will decline as your new fish dine out on this natural buffet. It is not enough to just establish your microfauna; you should actively protect their population too. Dense planting and botanicals provide hiding spots to protect your microfauna from predators.

Animals

A full account of aquarium botanicals is beyond the scope of this book, but it is worth knowing the basics. Botanicals are natural organics (e.g. leaves, twigs, and seedpods) that an aquarist introduces to their aquarium. This is typically done to achieve a natural 'blackwater' aesthetic – a rich tannin-stained water colour. For an organic aquarium – much like a botanical method aquarium – botanicals are more than just aesthetics. In these ecosystems, they are used to provide a nutrient-rich food source and an ideal habitat for our detrital crew. It is a method, not a style.

Commonly sold botanicals include dried almond and oak leaf, but there is a wide range of suitable options you can gather yourself. Research plant species local to you and find out what is suitable for aquarium use. Once you have a list of species, go foraging in an unpolluted area. There is a guide on preparing botanicals for your aquarium in the How-to section. If you do not have access to clean areas to source botanicals from, then it is recommended to get them online from a botanical aquarium specialist such as Betta Botanicals®.

Whilst the idea of adding sticks and leaf litter to your aquarium can be daunting, the biodiversity it nurtures is worth the effort.

HOW DO I ADD ANIMALS SAFELY?

Proper acclimation is very important when adding new animals to your aquarium. Even small differences in temperature, pH, or hardness can be stressful, or even deadly, if the transition is too sudden. Take it slow to give your fish or invertebrates the best chance of settling in.

Here's a step-by-step acclimation guide:

1. **Float the bag.** Turn off your aquarium light to reduce stress, then float the sealed transport bag in your tank for 20–30 minutes to match temperatures. If space is limited (e.g. in nano tanks), transfer the animal and its transport water into a smaller, clean container and float that securely in the aquarium.
2. **Add tank water slowly.** Open the bag or container and

gradually add small amounts of your tank water; about 50–100 ml every 10 minutes. You may need to remove some of the transport water before adding your own. Continue for about an hour until most of the water in the container is from your aquarium.
3. **Transfer with a net.** Gently net the fish or invertebrate and place it into your tank. Do not pour the transport water into your aquarium, as it may contain contaminants.

After introducing new animals, wait 12–24 hours before feeding or turning the light back on. Keep a close eye on them for the next few days and watch for any signs of stress. A careful start makes all the difference.

WHAT SHOULD I FEED THEM?

FEEDING THE FISH AND FERTILISING THE PLANTS

Feed once or twice a day, offering only as much as your fish can finish in a few minutes. Too much uneaten food can accumulate and rot, overloading the system. Start with modest feeds, then a couple of times a week, sprinkle in a little extra to help support plant growth. Whether it's eaten and excreted or left uneaten, the waste becomes a vital source of nutrients for your ecosystem. Just be sure your tank is handling it well.

Use high-quality, easily digestible foods as your staple. Flake food suited to your fish is ideal as it is nutritious and easily crushed into smaller pieces. Avoid cheap, filler-heavy foods that offer poor nutrition and create more mess. Good food creates good waste: rich in nutrients, low in pollution.

Variety is important too. A mix of food types provides a broader range of nutrients for your plants and enrichment for your fish. Occasional treats like live brine shrimp encourage natural foraging behaviour. As your tank matures, fish and shrimp will graze on natural food sources like algae, biofilm, and microfauna. This is one of the strengths of an organic system: a living food web that supplements your feeding.

Once again, feeding is another element of an organic aquarium which is governed by balance: enough to nourish your animals and fertilise your plants, but never so much that the system can't keep up.

FEEDING THE CLEANERS

Snails and shrimp spend their days grazing on detritus, biofilm, and algae, but they benefit from occasional supplements to stay healthy and active. Blanched vegetables like courgette, spinach, or carrot are favourites. These provide excellent nutrition (rich in minerals like calcium) and introduce additional organic matter into the system in a controlled way. There is a step-by-step guide on preparing spinach for your aquarium in the How-to section.

Botanicals, as mentioned earlier, are another natural food source. As they decay, they release tannins and grow biofilm, providing natural grazing for shrimp and snails. This mimics a natural stream where leaves fall in and the detrital food web benefits.

Lastly, if you have algae-eating fish in your aquarium, such as otocinclus, it is worth supplementing their diet with algae wafers. These can be added 1–2 times a week and provide an extra boost of nutrition for these helpful cleaners.

> **DISCLAIMER:** Research each species' specific habitat, water parameters, space requirements, and social needs before acquisition – never choose animals based solely on appearance if your system cannot meet their needs. Provide appropriate tank size, compatible tankmates, proper nutrition, and environmental enrichment for each species' wellbeing. Understand the long-term commitment, including adult size, lifespan, and care requirements. Plan responsibly for rehoming if circumstances change and never release non-native species into local waterways. Your ethical choices ensure the health and happiness of the animals in your care while supporting responsible aquarium practices.

7

Setting Up Your Aquarium

SHOPPING LIST

EQUIPMENT

TANK

☐ Container – a clean glass vessel

LIGHT

☐ Adjustable desk lamp
☐ 15–23W CFL daylight bulb
☐ Plug-in timer for 'siesta' schedule

SUBSTRATE

☐ Soil substrate – organic potting soil or topsoil without added fertilisers
☐ Cap – coarse sand (0.5–2 mm) or fine gravel (2–3 mm)

PLANTS

☐ Floating plants (e.g. duckweed, frogbit)
☐ Root-feeding plants (e.g. crypts, swords)

How to Create an Organic Aquarium

- ☐ Water-column feeders (e.g. hornwort, bacopa)
- ☐ Epiphytes and mosses (e.g. Java fern, anubias, Java moss)

WATER

- ☐ Reliable water source
- ☐ Water conditioner – to remove chlorine/chloramine
- ☐ Liquid test kit (ammonia, nitrite, nitrate, pH, GH/KH)
- ☐ Thermometer

MAINTENANCE

- ☐ Clean 5-gallon bucket (aquarium use only)
- ☐ Plastic tubing for water changes
- ☐ Scissors (aquarium or clean kitchen scissors)
- ☐ Aquarium net
- ☐ Plastic card, or a razor blade scraper – to shape soil and clean glass
- ☐ A clean cloth or kitchen roll – for cleaning the glass during setup
- ☐ Spray bottle – to keep plants moist during setup

EXTRAS

CONDITIONAL

- ☐ Heater
- ☐ Small filter/pump

OPTIONAL

- ☐ Spoon or cup – for distributing soil and cap
- ☐ Measuring stick or ruler – for measuring soil and cap depth
- ☐ Hardscape (rocks, driftwood, or decor)

Setting Up Your Aquarium

- ☐ Aquarium-safe superglue (cyanoacrylate gel) – for securing hardscape and attaching epiphytes and mosses
- ☐ Planting tweezers – for planting and propagating

THE PREP

POSITIONING YOUR AQUARIUM

You want to interact with your ecosystem regularly. Find a location where you can easily observe and maintain it.

Position it on a sturdy, level surface. Water weighs approximately 1 kilogram per litre – plus substrate, plus hardscape. Ensure your surface can support this load. Make sure the aquarium is in its final location before beginning the build: a filled tank should not be moved.

If you are using a second-hand tank, fill it and leave it for several hours to make sure it holds water. You do not want to spend hours creating a beautiful aquascape only to find the tank's seams don't hold water.

The light, heater, and filter need power, but all aquariums occasionally splash. Place your aquarium near outlets but far away enough to avoid splashing risks. Similarly, choose a location where spills won't damage furniture or flooring.

The aquarium's position should be away from direct sunlight, drafts, radiators, or air conditioners. The surface it is on should also be resistant to temperature swings (e.g. wood rather than stone). We want to create stable conditions; these factors can all cause temperature fluctuations and excessive algae growth.

SETTING UP YOUR LIGHTING

Before planting your aquarium, it is important to set up your light. The interplay of light and shade have a big effect on the look of your aquarium. This is an aesthetic and practical consideration. If your hardscape casts most of the tank in shade, your plants are going to struggle.

As a starting point, position your lamp so that the light source sits 15–20 cm above the top of the tank. This can be adjusted later based on plant response. Make sure that the light is evenly distributed across the aquarium.

Prepare the plug-in timer for its 'siesta' lighting schedule (4 hours on, 4 hours off, then 4 hours on) to balance plant growth and discourage algae. This can be connected at the end once your aquarium is assembled. In the meantime, just plug in the lamp and use the light to guide your hardscape and planting.

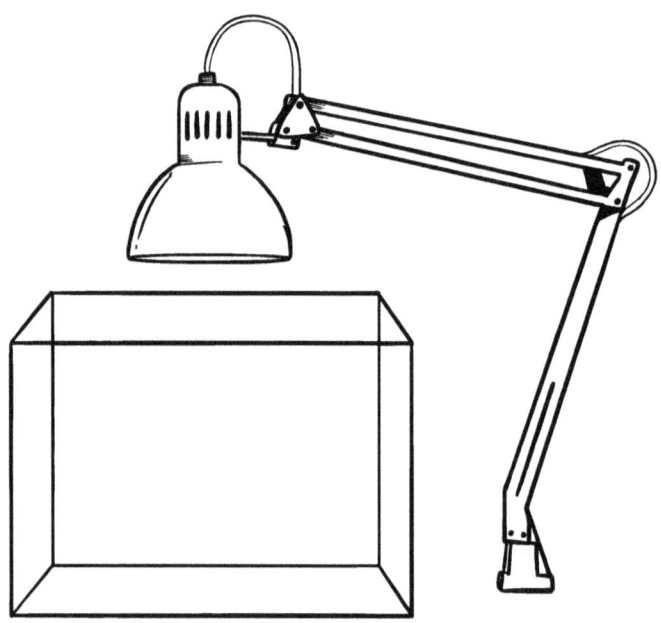

PLANNING YOUR LAYOUT

Find an inspiration, then keep it simple.

Research natural environments: riverbanks, lakeshores, forest streams. Look at how plants, hardscape, and light interact in these habitats. Aquarists of all abilities and budgets share their aquascapes online and it is a brilliant resource for ideas. There is a list of recommended forums and YouTube channels at the end of this book to get you started.

Setting Up Your Aquarium

Here are some key design principles to help guide your layout:
- Create asymmetrical compositions (odd numbers of rocks look more natural).
- Establish focal points with larger elements (the rule of thirds helps position these).
- Include negative space for visual relief and fish swimming areas.

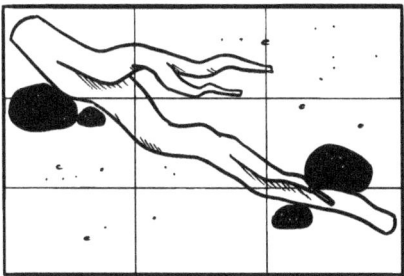 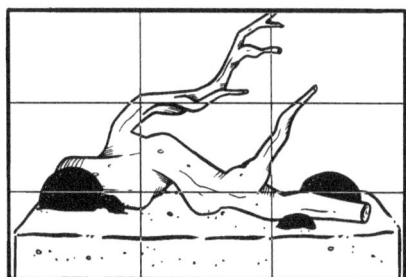

Once you have your hardscape, you can start to experiment with various dry arrangements. Use the aquarium box, or mark out the tank's dimensions with tape, as a size guide. Alternatively, you can temporarily fill your aquarium with your cap material and test different designs inside the aquarium. Adding the cap material at this stage protects the bottom of your tank and holds the hardscape in place as you experiment. With the aquarium lighting in place, you will get a much better understanding of how the finished result will look. Just note that you will have to remove the sand or gravel before proceeding with the build.

Photograph different arrangements as you experiment and see which composition you like the most. If you are undecided, step away for a day or two. See which composition you are most drawn to when you return. It is easier to spend time iterating with dry arrangements than it is once the tank is planted.

Don't overthink the design process. The most important thing to remember is that it is your tank. If you like the way it looks, you've succeeded.

Once you have decided on your layout, you are ready to start building.

THE BUILD

SUBSTRATE

ADDING THE SOIL

Prepare and portion the soil; be careful to distribute it at a consistent depth:
- Under 10 gallons: 2 cm depth
- 10–40-gallons: 2.5 cm depth
- 40 gallons and up with big plants: Up to 4 cm depth.

When distributing this layer, place less soil in areas that will be covered by hardscape.

Once in the aquarium, wet the soil with dechlorinated water until saturated (this makes it easier to manage during the capping). Then, use a plastic card to create a 2.5 cm gap between the soil and the aquarium walls. Lastly, clean any soil residue from the glass.

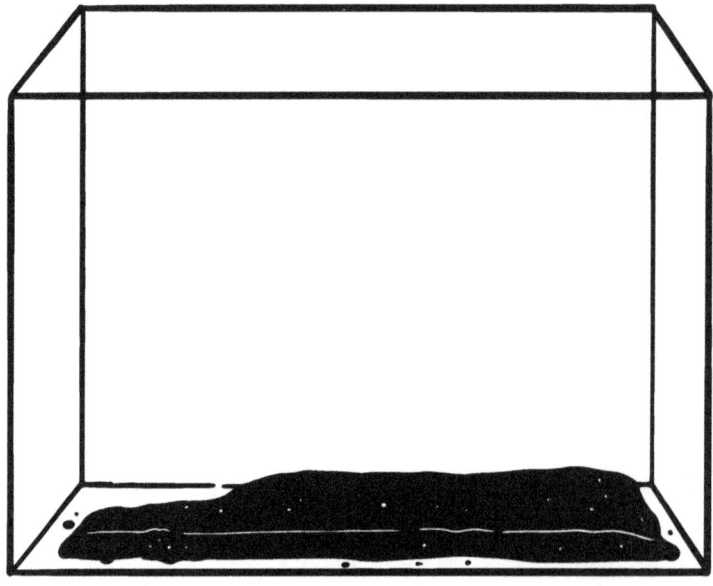

Setting Up Your Aquarium

CAPPING THE SOIL

Clean your cap material before adding it (this can be done ahead of time). The easiest way to do this is to add your cap to the bucket and fill it with water. Stir the cap material by hand and drain the cloudy water away. Repeat this until the water runs clear. Whatever dust and dirt you remove at this step is what you would otherwise have introduced into your aquarium.

When adding the cap, start by filling the gap between the soil and the aquarium walls; this will prevent the soil from being pushed into this clean area you've just created. Repeat for the areas with less soil cleared for hardscape. Once filled, gently cover the soil with a uniform layer:

- Coarse sand (0.5–2 mm): 2.5 cm depth
- Fine gravel (2–3 mm): 3.5–4 cm depth.

Check your substrate depth as you build to make sure you are building to your desired soil and cap measurements.

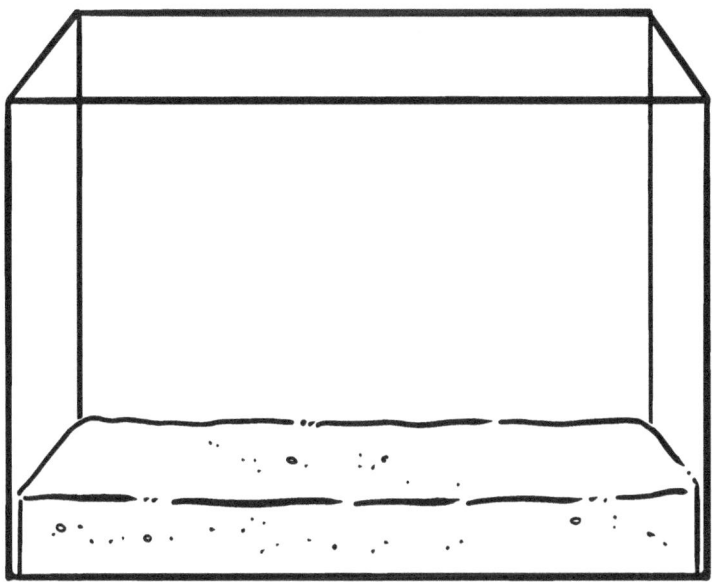

HARDSCAPE

With your substrate in place, you can now finish your layout. Be mindful to position the hardscape in the areas designated so that you don't compact or disrupt any soil.

If you are using driftwood, make sure it is waterlogged or attached to rocks to hold it in place. If the driftwood floats when the aquarium is filled, it can disrupt the layers of the substrate and pull soil into the water column.

If you are using rocks, make sure they are stable. If they wobble when tapped, reinforce them. This can be easily done by superglueing elements together at key contact points. If an unstable rock falls in your aquarium, it can easily break the glass and cause disaster. Better safe than sorry.

Once in place, you can enhance the layout with smaller stones, detail rocks, or thin pieces of wood to tie the whole scene together. By adding a variety of stone fragments, especially around larger hardscape elements, you can visually connect the cap to its surrounding environment.

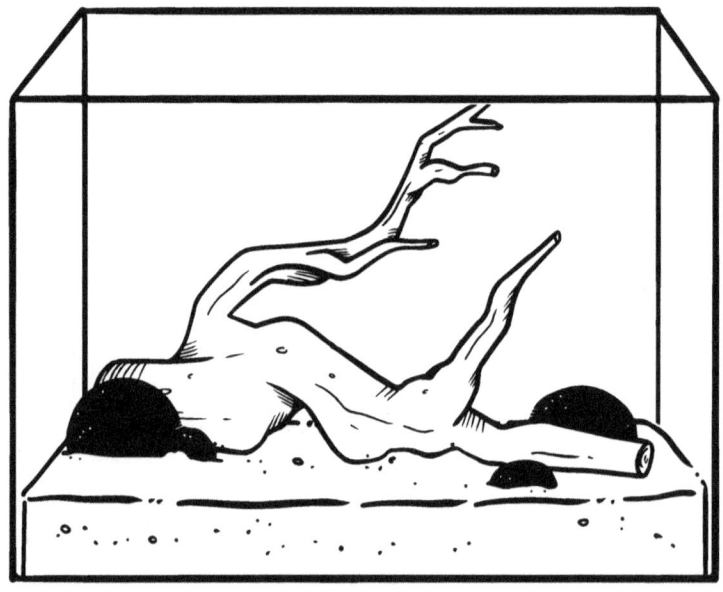

PLANTS

Heavy planting from day one is the best way to set your aquarium up for success. Aim for at least 50% coverage immediately to stabilise the aquarium environment quickly.

Prepare your plants for planting by removing their packaging and cleaning them gently. Trim away any damaged or dying leaves. You can also trim excessively long roots but only if required; it is best to preserve as much of the root as possible. Mist plants with dechlorinated water during planting to prevent them from drying out and maintain moisture until the aquarium is filled.

Start by attaching the epiphytes and mosses to the hardscape. Place epiphytes securely by wedging them into place, or by attaching the rhizome to the hardscape with aquarium-safe superglue. Similarly, mosses can be attached to smaller stones or directly to hardscape by using a thin layer of glue. When using superglue to attach plants to hardscape, less is more. You only need a small amount of glue as a contact point; too much can smother the rhizome.

Once the epiphytes and mosses are in place and secure (and the glue is drying), we can start planting in layers. Plant deeply into the substrate: ensure the base of the plant is pushed through the cap layer and into the soil below. Plant small species in the foreground, and taller plants in the midground and background.

The fast-growing water column feeders can be planted last, once the aquarium is filled. It is much easier to see how they sit in the aquarium once you can see them in their full height.

WATER

Once you have finished planting, treat your water according to the conditioner's instructions and fill your aquarium gradually until the water level is approximately 2.5 cm from the top. (In larger tanks, water conditioner can often be added directly to the tank to make filling easier.) It is important to not disturb the substrate layers when adding water. Place your hand, a clean sponge, or a piece of bubble wrap onto the substrate and pour water slowly onto it. This will displace the water and prevent it from

disrupting the cap and soil below.

Once filled, check to make sure your substrate, hardscape, and plants have not been disturbed. Plant the remaining stem-plants and any uprooted plants – you can use small stones to temporarily hold them in place if they stubbornly keep floating up.

At this stage, mount any additional equipment. If you are using a filter or water pump, wait for any initial cloudiness in the water to pass, then install. The outflow should be placed low to reduce surface agitation, and the flow rate should be minimal. Just enough to ensure a gentle circulation of the water throughout the aquarium. If you are using a heater, ensure it is positioned where it will not be smothered by plants or hardscape. If there is a filter or water pump in the aquarium, place the heater close to the filter outflow. This will help distribute the heat evenly throughout the system.

Lastly, spread the floating plants across the water's surface, making sure they are all the right way up. If you are eager to try houseplant hydroponics, this is the perfect time to add them.

THE BALANCE

INITIAL WATER CHANGE

Within 24 hours of setup, perform a 50–75% water change. This significant water replacement helps clear initial cloudiness and tannins released from the substrate and hardscape, ensuring clearer water for observing your aquarium's development. Refill gently with dechlorinated water to avoid disturbing plants and substrate.

For the next 4 weeks, refrain from performing any further water changes. This period allows the biological processes to stabilise and beneficial microbes to establish a balanced ecosystem naturally.

If some plants die or melt causing coverage to drop below 50%, add more floating and fast-growing species to prevent algae from gaining the advantage. If you are starting with under 50% plant coverage, perform small water changes (10–25%) twice a week for the first 4 weeks and propagate fast-growing species.

TIMELINE

- **Weeks 0–4 (Pioneer):** Expect initial cloudiness, biofilm growth, and early algae blooms such as brown diatoms. These initial signs are natural and indicative of biological activity. Do not introduce any animals during this stage. Let plants establish themselves and microbes colonise the aquarium.
- **Weeks 4–8 (Intermediate):** Monitor water parameters closely. Once ammonia and nitrite levels remain consistently at zero, introduce your hardy clean-up crew: shrimp and snails. These organisms will help manage algae, detritus, and biofilm, supporting the detrital food web.
- **Week 8 onwards (Climax):** If water parameters remain stable (i.e. ammonia and nitrite stay at zero) and plants are growing healthily, slowly introduce fish. Add fish in small groups and monitor water quality closely after each addition to ensure the biological filtration adjusts to increased bioload without disturbance.

TESTING

Test water parameters regularly (ammonia, nitrite, nitrate, pH, GH/KH) to confirm stable, healthy conditions. Test every few days in the pioneer stage; every other day in the intermediate stage; and every day in the first couple of weeks of the climax stage (after introducing fish). Consistent testing allows prompt detection and management of potential imbalances, ensuring your aquarium remains a thriving, balanced ecosystem.

8

Maintenance

HOW DO I MAINTAIN AN ORGANIC AQUARIUM?

The beauty of this method lies in trusting natural processes rather than imposing rigid maintenance schedules. As Lowenfels writes:

Through intervention, the farmer risks damaging a crucial niche within the web. This can cause the web to operate imperfectly, creating a vicious cycle of increasing interventions[33].

Understand that your role is not to micromanage, but to guide development and learn from responses. Through patient observation and minimal intervention, you'll develop an intuitive understanding of your aquarium's rhythms.

We have already covered roles of plant pruning, cleaning the glass, and water changes in our discussion of essential equipment. There are, however, a few more tasks to undertake to ensure our aquarium stays on the right path.

DAILY AND WEEKLY TASKS

Each day, start with observation. Take a moment to check your tank: is the water clear? Are your fish active and feeding well? Are your plants putting out new growth? These small visual cues can tell you a lot about the overall health of your system.

Next, check your equipment. Make sure the water temperature is steady, the filter or pump is circulating water gently, and the lights are running on their regular cycle. These quiet background systems keep your aquarium stable, so it's worth confirming they're working as expected.

Pay attention to detritus buildup on the substrate. One simple way to tell if there's too much is to watch how quickly food disappears. If leftovers from the morning's feeding are still sitting on the bottom by evening, skip the next feed and check again the following night. If food is still there, it's a sign your system may be overloaded with organics. In that case, perform a small water change (10–25%) and gently siphon away excess detritus. This soft reset helps restore balance and keeps waste from turning into toxic ammonia spikes.

Every few days, test your water. In the first few months, it's important to regularly check ammonia, nitrite, nitrate, pH, GH, and KH. If you detect ammonia or nitrite after the first 4 weeks, do a 25–50% water change. Once your system has stabilised, you can reduce testing frequency. Keeping a simple log of results and observations helps you track trends and spot problems early.

Once a week, top up any evaporated water using dechlorinated tap water. You can also take this time to prune fast-growing plants and gently spot-clean any algae from the glass if needed.

All of this takes just a few minutes, but these regular check-ins go a long way. They help you stay in tune with your tank's natural rhythms and keep your aquarium running smoothly.

MONTHLY AND QUARTERLY TASKS

While daily care keeps things running smoothly, longer-term maintenance helps your aquarium stay healthy as it matures. These occasional check-ins let you spot slow changes and step in before they become problems.

Every few months, consider whether your tank might benefit from a partial water change. If water parameters are stable and plants are thriving, there's no need to intervene. But if nitrates begin to rise, or something feels off, a small water change (10–25%) can help reset the balance. Always use dechlorinated water, match the temperature, and add gradually to avoid shocking your fish or stirring the substrate.

If you use a filter, clean it when you do your water change. Rinse sponges or mechanical media in old tank water (not tap water as it will kill beneficial bacteria) and make sure the outlets are clear.

Plant maintenance also shifts as your system ages. Fast growers may need trimming every couple of weeks, but every few months you may want to replant new cuttings or thin out crowded areas. This prevents nutrient bottlenecks in dense patches and spreads new growth to different areas of the soil. Keep an eye out for signs of decay too; if there are a lot of dead or melting leaves, they should be removed before they overwhelm the system.

Once your tank is over 2 years old, it's worth assessing the soil itself every few months. Most organic substrates provide nutrients for 2 to 3 years, but this depends on how heavily the tank is planted and stocked. As discussed earlier in the book, you'll know the soil is nearing the end of its life when rooted plants begin to fade or stop growing, despite good lighting and stable water conditions. At that point, consider adding root tabs beneath your hungriest plants, or even rebuilding the aquarium with fresh soil. If you decide to start again, you will need somewhere to house your fish and invertebrates whilst your new aquarium stabilises.

Just like in nature, long-term balance is built on small seasonal shifts. These occasional tasks help you stay in step with your tank's slow rhythms and ensure it continues to flourish over time.

WHAT IF I DON'T KNOW WHAT TO DO?

Organic systems are complex, dynamic, and remarkably resilient, but challenges will still occasionally arise. Don't hesitate to ask for help. Online communities of soil-based aquarium keepers are generous with their knowledge and experience.

One of the best habits you can build early on is simple observation paired with light record-keeping. You don't need spreadsheets or special apps, just some way of keeping notes and a weekly photo of your aquarium taken from the same angle. Together, these simple tools can help you spot patterns that might otherwise go unnoticed. If something feels off and you're unsure why, sharing photos and a timeline of your observations can make all the difference.

Make quick notes of your water test results, and jot down anything unusual during daily checks: colour changes in plants or fish, shifts in water clarity, new algae growth, or odd behaviour. Record the dates of any actions you take – like pruning, water changes, or equipment tweaks. These notes become valuable reference points over time.

If you run into an issue, there's a good chance someone else has faced it, and hopefully even solved it. Reach out. Ask questions. Share your successes and setbacks. You don't need to be an expert to contribute something useful.

Conclusion

A GROWING COMMUNITY

One of the many rewards of keeping an organic aquarium is seeing what happens when you step back and let nature lead. You start with soil, water, and plants – and, with time, an ecosystem emerges.

And you're not doing this alone.

This approach has been adopted by a growing community of aquarists who value natural processes and learning through observation. It's shaped by curiosity. There is a mix of beginners and long-time hobbyists, all asking questions, sharing what works, and often sharing what didn't. It's a generous space, and it grows when people contribute. You'll find them in social media groups, online forums, and local aquarium shops trading notes on plants, soil, light, and life.

If someone you know might enjoy this approach, someone who loves nature or who is simply looking for a quiet project, why not invite them to try it too? Watching multiple tanks evolve side by side, each shaped by different choices and conditions, is one of the most engaging ways to deepen your understanding of these intricate worlds.

Ready to see what grows?

Scan this code to download and share an introductory **Quick Start Guide**. *The step-by-step tutorial shows how to build a no-tech shrimp jar using the organic method. While it doesn't explore the method in full detail (that is what this book is for!), it is a great starting point for anyone curious about aquariums.*

How-to Guides

CULTURING WILD MICROFAUNA

MATERIALS

- Decomposing leaves from a stream or pond
- Small watertight container – for transport
- Large container (at least 1 litre) – for culturing
- Breathable material – to cover the large container
- Rubber band or tape – to secure the breathable material
- Tap water conditioner
- Pipette

PREPARATION

1. Using the watertight container, gather some decomposing leaves and a small amount of water from a clean stream or pond.
2. Once home, add them to the large container and top up with dechlorinated water.
3. Cover the container with the breathable material and secure it in place – this contains the inhabitants whilst allowing gas exchange.

INSTRUCTIONS

Once the large container has been prepared, position it in an area with indirect sunlight and a stable temperature. Over the next 4 weeks, you should see microfauna appear and multiply.

As this culture establishes, you can use a pipette to isolate desirable microfauna (e.g. daphnia or seed shrimp) and introduce them to your aquarium. If you choose to culture a wild sample, ensure you check local regulations and obtain necessary permissions before collecting.

ADDING BOTANICALS TO YOUR AQUARIUM

MATERIALS

- Dead and dried botanicals suitable for aquarium use
- Cooking pot
- Colander
- Clean container
- Tap water conditioner

PREPARATION

1. Rinse the botanicals thoroughly.
2. Add them to a pot of boiling water for 5 minutes.
3. Drain and strain the botanicals and add them to the container.
4. Soak the botanicals in dechlorinated water until waterlogged.
5. Your botanicals are ready to be added to your aquarium.

INSTRUCTIONS

Once prepped, your botanicals are ready to be added to your aquarium – but add them gradually. If you introduce a large amount of leaf litter all at once you can overwhelm your system. By adding them piece by piece over the course a few days or weeks, you give the system (and yourself) time to react. If you notice unusual behaviour from your aquarium's inhabitants, remove the botanicals and perform a 25–50% water change.

REPLACEMENT

Your detrital crew will eventually process the leaves, so you will have to add more over time to ensure they stay sheltered, but this is all part of the process. Eventually you will create a natural habitat supporting a variety of microfauna, even with hungry fish patrolling for critter-shaped snacks.

BLANCHING SPINACH AS A SUPPLEMENT

MATERIALS

- Fresh spinach leaves
- Kettle or pot to boil water
- Heat-safe mug or bowl
- Paper towel
- Feeding clip or small stone

PREPARATION

1. Rinse spinach thoroughly.
2. Place the spinach in a heat-safe mug or bowl.
3. Adding boiling water to the spinach until fully submerged.
4. Let it steep for 5 minutes so the leaves become dark green and limp.
5. Remove spinach, let it cool and pat dry.

INSTRUCTIONS

- Clip portion to aquarium glass or weigh down using a small inert stone.
- Remove uneaten portions after 12–24 hours.
- Use as supplement to regular fish nutrition.

NUTRIENT BENEFIT NOTE

In organic soil-based aquariums, potassium and iron are the first to be depleted from the water column, even when other nutrients remain available. Blanched spinach offers a natural source of these elements and benefits both your animals and plants when introduced in moderation.

VEGETABLE PREPARATION NOTE

Purchase organic vegetables to minimise pesticide exposure to aquatic life. Always peel vegetables such as courgette and cucumber before feeding.

Field Guide

Plants

 **Aerial advantage:** This plant can use atmospheric carbon dioxide. Plants which can use atmospheric carbon dioxide but only in high humidity (e.g. mosses) have not been labelled with 'aerial advantage', as this is difficult to achieve in an open-topped aquarium.

 **Bicarbonate:** This plant can break bicarbonates in hardwater as an alternative carbon dioxide source.

PLANTS:
Floating plants

AERIAL ADVANTAGE

AZOLLA CAROLINIANA (MOSQUITO FERN)

Azollaceae

Native habitat & ecology

- Region: Tropical to temperate zones worldwide
- Habitat: Still or slow-moving freshwater bodies including ponds, canals, and wetlands

Role

Fast-growing, nitrogen-fixing floater that absorbs excess nutrients, provides microhabitat for fry and microorganisms, and offers partial shade that suppresses algae without blocking all light.

Physical characteristics

- Form & Size: Tiny, floating fern; forms velvet-like surface mats
- Colour: Green to reddish depending on light intensity
- Growth Rate: Very fast; can double biomass every 5–7 days

Water parameters

- Temperature: 15–30°C
- pH: 6.5–8.0
- Hardness: 0–18 dGH

Tank requirements

- Position: Floating, surface layer
- Lighting: Medium to high; turns red under intense light
- Substrate: N/A

Maintenance & care

- Routine care: Weekly thinning recommended
- Potential issues:
  - Clings to equipment and plants
  - Difficult to fully remove
  - May be eaten by some fish species

LEMNA MINOR (COMMON DUCKWEED)

Araceae

Native habitat & ecology

- Region: Global distribution; found on every continent except Antarctica
- Habitat: Still or slow-moving freshwater bodies including ponds, canals, and wetlands

Role

Ultra-fast-growing surface plant that absorbs nitrates and phosphates directly from the water column, provides cover for fry, and helps suppress algae by reducing light penetration. Also serves as a supplemental food source for some herbivorous fish.

Physical characteristics

- Form & Size: Tiny, free-floating plant with 1–3 oval fronds and a single trailing root
- Colour: Bright green; stays consistent across light levels
- Growth Rate: Extremely fast; can double in mass every 2–4 days in nutrient-rich conditions

Water parameters

- Temperature: 15–30°C
- pH: 6.5–7.5
- Hardness: 2–20 dGH

Tank requirements

- Position: Floating, surface layer
- Lighting: Low to high; tolerates a wide range
- Substrate: N/A

Maintenance & care

- Routine care: Remove excess weekly or as needed to maintain light and gas exchange
- Potential issues:
    - Can block all surface light if unchecked
    - Extremely difficult to eradicate once established
    - May clog filters or stick to equipment

LIMNOBIUM LAEVIGATUM (AMAZON FROGBIT)

Hydrocharitaceae

Native habitat & ecology

- Region: Central and South America
- Habitat: Still or slow-moving freshwater bodies including ponds, canals, and wetlands

Role

Large-rooted floating plant that absorbs excess nutrients from the water column, creates shaded areas that inhibit algae, and offers microhabitat for fry and surface-dwelling invertebrates.

Physical characteristics

- Form & Size: Rosette-forming floater with thick, buoyant leaves and long, dangling roots
- Colour: Bright green leaves with spongy undersides; roots can extend 10–20 cm
- Growth Rate: Medium to fast; slower than duckweed or Azolla but still requires regular thinning

Water parameters

- Temperature: 18–28°C
- pH: 6.0–7.5
- Hardness: 2–12 dGH

Tank requirements

- Position: Floating, surface layer
- Lighting: Medium; broader leaves form under higher light
- Substrate: N/A

Maintenance & care

- Routine care: Weekly removal of excess plants and occasional root trimming to prevent entanglement
- Potential issues:
    - Sensitive to water splashing; leaves rot if constantly wet
    - Long roots may entangle submerged plants or clog filters
    - May develop chlorosis if micronutrients (especially iron) are lacking

AERIAL ADVANTAGE

PHYLLANTHUS FLUITANS (RED ROOT FLOATER)

Phyllanthaceae

Native habitat & ecology

- Region: South America (Amazon River basin)
- Habitat: Calm backwaters, floodplains, and oxbow lakes with soft, nutrient-rich water

Role

Striking floating plant that provides surface shade, improves water quality through nutrient absorption, and offers refuge for fry beneath its dense root curtain.

Physical characteristics

- Form & Size: Small, heart-shaped floating leaves with trailing crimson roots
- Colour: Green to red leaves depending on light and nutrients; vivid red roots
- Growth Rate: Fast; rapidly forms surface mats under stable conditions

Water parameters

- Temperature: 20–30°C
- pH: 6.5–7.5
- Hardness: 4–12 dGH

Tank requirements

- Position: Floating, surface layer
- Lighting: Moderate to high; high light encourages red colouration
- Substrate: N/A

Maintenance & care

- Routine care: Regular thinning and removal of deteriorating leaves to maintain surface access and plant health
- Potential issues:
  - Can overgrow and block light to submerged plants
  - Sensitive to splashing and strong surface agitation
  - May exhibit chlorosis or dull colour without adequate iron

PISTIA STRATIOTES (WATER LETTUCE)

Araceae

Native habitat & ecology

- Region: Tropical and subtropical zones worldwide
- Habitat: Still or slow-moving freshwater bodies including ponds, canals, and wetlands

Role

Large, rosette-forming floater that absorbs excess nitrogen and phosphorus, shades the water surface to reduce algae, and provides extensive microhabitat within its long trailing roots.

Physical characteristics

- Form & Size: Rosette-forming plant with soft, velvety leaves; roots trail beneath like a dense beard
- Colour: Pale to bright green, depending on light and nutrients
- Growth Rate: Fast under warm, nutrient-rich conditions

Water parameters

- Temperature: 20–28°C
- pH: 6.5–7.5
- Hardness: 4–12 dGH

Tank requirements

- Position: Floating, surface layer
- Lighting: Medium to high; thrives with bright, indirect light
- Substrate: N/A

Maintenance & care

- Routine care: Weekly thinning and root trimming recommended
- Potential issues:
  - Large rosettes can block light from reaching submerged plants
  - Sensitive to water movement; leaves may rot if splashed
  - Not suitable for small aquariums due to size and shading effect

SALVINIA MINIMA (WATER SPANGLES)

Salviniaceae

Native habitat & ecology

- Region: Central and South America
- Habitat: Still or slow-moving freshwater bodies including ponds, canals, and wetlands

Role

Rapid-growing floating fern that absorbs excess nutrients, suppresses algae through surface shading, and provides a gentle light-diffusing canopy ideal for fry and shade-adapted species.

Floating Plants

Physical characteristics

- Form & Size: Small floating fern with oval, water-repellent leaves that form a distinctive egg-beater texture
- Colour: Bright green; may darken under intense light or nutrient saturation
- Growth Rate: Fast; capable of doubling in surface area every 3–4 days under optimal conditions

Water parameters

- Temperature: 18–30°C
- pH: 6.0–8.0
- Hardness: 2–20 dGH

Tank requirements

- Position: Floating, surface layer
- Lighting: Medium to high; tolerates lower light but grows more slowly
- Substrate: N/A

Maintenance & care

- Routine care: Remove excess growth weekly to prevent full surface coverage
- Potential issues:
    - Can block light if allowed to cover entire surface
    - May clog filters or pumps if not contained
    - Dies back quickly if submerged or caught beneath water surface

PLANTS:
Root-feeding plants

CRYPTOCORYNE WENDTII

Araceae

Native habitat & ecology

- Region: Asia (Sri Lanka)
- Habitat: Shaded streams and riverbanks with fluctuating water levels and nutrient-rich substrates

Root-feeding Plants

Role

Hardy rosette-forming root feeder that stabilises the substrate, prevents anaerobic zones, and adapts well to variable water chemistry – ideal for newly established or low-tech tanks.

Physical characteristics

- Form & Size: Compact rosettes with ruffled, lanceolate leaves; varies in colour from green to bronze to deep brown
- Colour: Depends on variety, lighting, and nutrient conditions
- Growth Rate: Slow; produces new leaves every 2–3 weeks once established

Water parameters

- Temperature: 22–28°C
- pH: 6.0–7.5
- Hardness: 2–12 dGH

Tank requirements

- Position: Foreground to midground, depending on variety
- Lighting: Low to medium; thrives in shaded areas
- Substrate: Requires nutrient-rich substrate or active soil

Maintenance & care

- Routine care: Remove damaged or melting leaves as needed; divide clumps annually if overcrowded
- Potential issues:
    - Prone to melting after transplanting or sudden environmental changes
    - Slow to recover from damage or disturbance
    - May stay dormant for weeks before resuming growth

ECHINODORUS AMAZONICUS (AMAZON SWORD)

Alismataceae

Native habitat & ecology

- Region: South America (Amazon River basin)
- Habitat: Shallow, slow-moving freshwater bodies with fluctuating water levels and nutrient-rich substrates

Root-feeding Plants

Role

Large, rooted background plant that anchors the substrate, draws nutrients from the soil, and provides shelter, spawning sites, and vertical structure in the aquascape.

Physical characteristics

- Form & Size: Dense rosette with long, sword-shaped leaves; can reach up to 30–50 cm in height
- Colour: Vibrant green; younger leaves may be lighter or slightly reddish
- Growth Rate: Moderate to fast; accelerates with rich substrate and stable conditions

Water parameters

- Temperature: 22–28°C
- pH: 6.5–7.5
- Hardness: 4–12 dGH

Tank requirements

- Position: Background or central focal point in larger aquariums
- Lighting: Medium to high
- Substrate: Requires nutrient-rich soil for long-term health

Maintenance & care

- Routine care: Trim older leaves to promote new growth and maintain access to light for surrounding plants
- Potential issues:
  - Can outgrow smaller tanks; best suited to tanks 20 gallons and above
  - Susceptible to iron deficiency in depleted soils
  - May shade out lower-growing or light-sensitive plants nearby

ECHINODORUS TENELLUS (PYGMY CHAIN SWORD)

Alismataceae

Native habitat & ecology

- Region: North and South America
- Habitat: Shallow margins of streams, rivers, and wetlands; often grows partially emersed in muddy or sandy substrates

Role

Compact foreground plant that forms dense runners, stabilises the substrate, oxygenates the soil, and supports nutrient cycling at the tank floor.

Physical characteristics

- Form & Size: Narrow, grass-like leaves; forms low-growing carpets via runners
- Colour: Bright green; may develop a reddish tint under high light
- Growth Rate: Moderate; spreads steadily with adequate nutrients and lighting

Water parameters

- Temperature: 20–28°C
- pH: 6.0–7.5
- Hardness: 2–15 dGH

Tank requirements

- Position: Foreground; carpeting plant
- Lighting: Medium to high; brighter light encourages horizontal growth and denser carpets
- Substrate: Requires fine-grain, nutrient-rich substrate or soil

Maintenance & care

- Routine care: Occasional trimming and removal of excess runners to control spread and maintain open areas
- Potential issues:
    - May grow leggy or upward in low light
    - Slower spread in nutrient-poor substrates
    - Can be shaded out by larger or floating plants

LUDWIGIA REPENS (RED LUDWIGIA)

Onagraceae

Native habitat & ecology

- Region: Central and North America
- Habitat: Tropical marshes, ponds, and slow-moving streams; capable of submerged and aerial growth

Root-feeding Plants

Role

Root-feeding stem plant that draws nutrients from soil and water, aiding substrate. With robust foliage, it stabilises ecosystems and adds dynamic structure and colour. Useful as a focal midground or background element.

Physical characteristics

- Form & Size: Tall, upright stems reaching 30–50 cm; forms bushy clusters
- Colour: Green to red/orange under strong light
- Growth Rate: Fast; fills space quickly with thick foliage

Water parameters

- Temperature: 20–28°C
- pH: 6.5–7.5
- Hardness: 4–12 dGH

Tank requirements

- Position: Midground to background
- Lighting: Low to moderate light yields green tones; bright light enhances red colouration
- Substrate: Prefers nutrient-rich soil; gravel acceptable with root tabs or dosing

Maintenance & care

- Routine care: Regular trimming maintains height and encourages bushier growth
- Potential issues:
  - Lower leaves may drop in low light or poor flow
  - Can shade or crowd neighbouring plants
  - Red colouration fades without sufficient light

SAGITTARIA SUBULATA (DWARF SAGITTARIA)

Alismataceae

Native habitat & ecology

- Region: South America
- Habitat: Coastal streams, estuaries, and shallow freshwater bodies with silty or sandy substrates

Role

Hardy carpeting plant that stabilises the substrate, prevents soil erosion, and provides cover for bottom-dwelling fish, shrimp, and spawning species.

Physical characteristics

- Form & Size: Narrow, grass-like leaves growing in small basal rosettes; spreads via runners
- Colour: Bright green
- Growth Rate: Moderate; forms carpets over time through horizontal spread

Water parameters

- Temperature: 20–28°C
- pH: 6.5–8.0
- Hardness: 8–12 dGH

Tank requirements

- Position: Foreground or midground, depending on lighting
- Lighting: Low to medium; adapts well to a range of light levels
- Substrate: Requires fine-grain, nutrient-rich substrate or soil

Maintenance & care

- Routine care: Trim or remove runners if carpeting becomes too dense or spreads into unwanted areas
- Potential issues:
    - Can grow taller than expected under lower light
    - May become invasive in nutrient-rich conditions
    - Dense growth may trap detritus between leaves

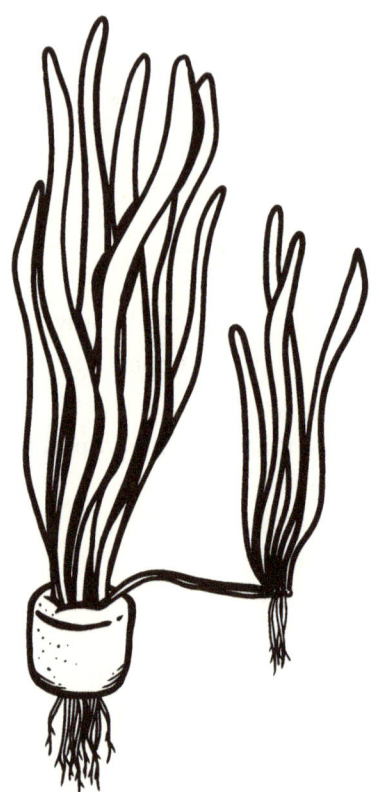

VALLISNERIA SPIRALIS (STRAIGHT VALLISNERIA)

Hydrocharitaceae

Native habitat & ecology

- Region: Widely distributed across Europe, Asia, and North Africa
- Habitat: Freshwater rivers, lakes, and canals with moderate flow and silty or sandy substrates

Role

Fast-growing background plant that oxygenates the substrate, stabilises soil, and provides vertical structure and cover for fish, shrimp, and fry.

Physical characteristics

- Form & Size: Ribbon-like, linear leaves growing from a central rosette; can reach 30–60 cm in height
- Colour: Bright to medium green
- Growth Rate: Moderate to fast; spreads via runners once established

Water parameters

- Temperature: 20–28°C
- pH: 6.5–8.0
- Hardness: 4–18 dGH

Tank requirements

- Position: Background
- Lighting: Low to high; grows in a wide range of lighting conditions
- Substrate: Requires fine to medium-grain substrate; grows best in nutrient-rich soil

Maintenance & care

- Routine care: Trim leaf tips as needed and remove excess runners to prevent crowding
- Potential issues:
    - Can quickly overtake smaller tanks if not controlled
    - Runners may disturb neighbouring plants
    - May develop calcium deposits on leaves in very hard water

PLANTS:
Water column feeders

BACOPA CAROLINIANA (GIANT BACOPA)

Plantaginaceae

Native habitat & ecology

- Region: North America
- Habitat: Margins of streams, ponds, wetlands, and ditches; capable of submerged and aerial growth

Role

Reliable, undemanding stem plant that contributes to water clarity by absorbing excess nutrients and stabilising tank chemistry through steady, predictable growth; its waxy leaves also allow it to put out aerial growth in open-top tanks.

Physical characteristics

- Form & Size: Upright stem plant with thick, rounded leaves arranged in opposite pairs
- Colour: Bright to olive green; stems can turn reddish under strong light
- Growth Rate: Moderate; produces new nodes steadily in stable conditions

Water parameters

- Temperature: 20–28°C
- pH: 6.0–7.5
- Hardness: 2–16 dGH

Tank requirements

- Position: Midground to background
- Lighting: Medium; tolerates lower light but may become leggy
- Substrate: Adaptable; benefits from nutrient-rich substrate

Maintenance & care

- Routine care: Trim tops regularly and replant cuttings to maintain bushy growth
- Potential issues:
  - Can become sparse or stretch in low light
  - May develop mineral deficiencies in very soft water
  - Slower growing than other stem plants; not ideal for nutrient spiking scenarios

CERATOPHYLLUM DEMERSUM (HORNWORT)

Ceratophyllaceae

Native habitat & ecology

- Region: Global distribution; found on every continent except Antarctica
- Habitat: Still or slow-moving freshwater lakes, ponds, and canals; often free-floating or loosely anchored in sediments

Water Column Feeders

Role

Exceptionally fast-growing oxygenator and nutrient sponge that absorbs ammonia, nitrate, and phosphate directly from the water column; ideal for stabilising new tanks and preventing algae outbreaks.

Physical characteristics

- Form & Size: Bushy, rootless plant with thin, forked leaves arranged in whorls around flexible stems
- Colour: Bright green to olive
- Growth Rate: Very fast; can grow 2 cm per day under favourable conditions

Water parameters

- Temperature: 15–30°C
- pH: 6.0–8.0
- Hardness: 4–20 dGH

Tank requirements

- Position: Floating or loosely anchored; adaptable
- Lighting: Low to high; very adaptable, though faster growth in higher light
- Substrate: Not required; can float freely or be gently weighed down

Maintenance & care

- Routine care: Trim excess growth weekly to maintain open swimming space and light penetration
- Potential issues:
    - May shed 'needles' when adjusting to new conditions or under nutrient stress
    - Can overgrow small tanks rapidly
    - Trimmings may clog filters if not removed promptly

HEMIANTHUS GLOMERATUS (PEARLWEED)

Linderniaceae

Native habitat & ecology

- Region: North America
- Habitat: Margins of streams, ponds, wetlands, and ditches

Role

Versatile and fast-growing stem plant that improves water quality by absorbing nutrients from the water column and substrate; provides dense cover for fry and serves as a natural aquascaping element for carpeting or bushy midground forms.

Physical characteristics

- Form & Size: Fine, branching stems with small, bright green leaves; forms dense bushes or carpets depending on trimming
- Colour: Bright green; compact under strong light
- Growth Rate: Fast; responds quickly to light and nutrients

Water parameters

- Temperature: 18–28°C
- pH: 6.0–7.5
- Hardness: 4–15 dGH

Tank requirements

- Position: Foreground (as carpet) or midground (as bushy mound)
- Lighting: Medium to high; intense light encourages compact growth
- Substrate: Grows best in nutrient-rich substrate but tolerates inert gravel with dosing

Maintenance & care

- Routine care: Frequent trimming needed to maintain shape; cuttings can be replanted to expand coverage
- Potential issues:
  - May grow leggy under low light
  - Can overshadow or crowd smaller plants
  - Trimmings may float and root in unintended areas

HYGROPHILA POLYSPERMA (INDIAN WATERWEED)

Acanthaceae

Native habitat & ecology

- Region: Asia (India, Bangladesh, China, Malaysia)
- Habitat: Inundated areas, marshes, and stream margins; capable of submerged and aerial growth

Role

- Versatile, fast-growing stem plant. Absorbs excess nutrients from both water column and substrate, helping prevent algae. Dense foliage provides cover for fry and visual depth. Ideal for early tank development and can be pruned to control spread.

Physical characteristics

- Form & Size: Upright, branching stems reaching up to 60 cm
- Colour: Bright green; often shifts to pink, orange, or red under strong light
- Growth Rate: Very fast; can grow up to 10 cm per week

Water parameters

- Temperature: 20–28°C
- pH: 5.0–8.0
- Hardness: 2–18 dGH

Tank requirements

- Position: Midground to background
- Lighting: Low to high; brighter light enhances colour and density
- Substrate: Thrives in nutrient-rich substrate but tolerates inert gravel

Maintenance & care

- Routine care: Trim stems frequently to maintain shape; cuttings easily replanted
- Potential issues:
    - Can overtake slower plants if not pruned
    - May lose lower leaves in low light
    - Pruned cuttings may root in unwanted areas

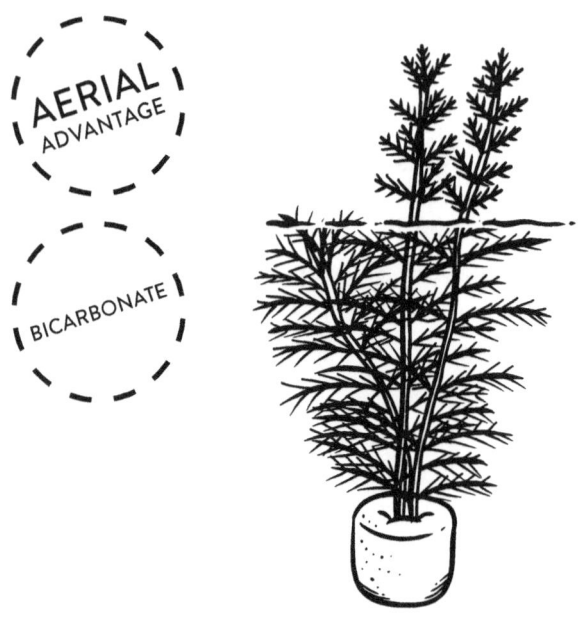

MYRIOPHYLLUM MATTOGROSSENSE (WATER MILFOIL)

Haloragaceae

Native habitat & ecology

- Region: South America (Brazil – Mato Grosso region)
- Habitat: Shallow, slow-moving rivers, floodplains, and lagoons with fluctuating water levels and nutrient-rich substrates; capable of submerged and aerial growth

Role

- Fast-growing, fine-leaved stem plant that acts as an effective nutrient sponge. Provides dense cover for fry, shrimp, and small fish, and its delicate texture adds contrast to coarser-leaved plants. Capable of aerial growth where it develops sturdier, thicker leaves. Resembles small pine trees.

Physical characteristics

- Form & Size: Whorled stems with finely divided, feathery submerged leaves; aerial growth produces simpler, more rigid leaf structures with reduced division and a stronger central stem
- Colour: Bright to medium green; may take on bronze hues under high light and nutrient-rich conditions
- Growth Rate: Moderate to fast

Water parameters

- Temperature: 20–28°C
- pH: 6.0–7.5
- Hardness: 4–16 dGH

Tank requirements

- Position: Midground to background
- Lighting: Low to high; brighter light enhances colour and density
- Substrate: Thrives in nutrient-rich substrate but obtains most nutrients from the water column

Maintenance & care

- Routine care: Regular trimming encourages lateral shoots and denser growth; stems can be replanted to propagate
- Potential issues:
  - Fine leaves can trap debris and algae if water movement is too low
  - Growth may become leggy in low light
  - Sensitive to prolonged shading from floating plants

ROTALA ROTUNDIFOLIA

Lythraceae

Native habitat & ecology

- Region: Asia (India, Vietnam, Thailand)
- Habitat: Flooded rice fields, ditches, and stream margins; capable of submerged and aerial growth

Role

Delicate stem plant that absorbs excess nutrients from the water column, stabilises tank chemistry, and contributes to aquascape aesthetics through its colour and form; readily transitions to aerial growth in shallow or open-top tanks while providing shelter for small fish and fry.

Physical characteristics

- Form & Size: Fine, branching stems with lanceolate leaves when submerged; small, rounded aerial growth
- Colour: Green to pink-orange; develops vivid red hues under high light
- Growth Rate: Fast; produces new growth rapidly with adequate light and nutrients

Water parameters

- Temperature: 22–28°C
- pH: 6.0–7.5
- Hardness: 2–12 dGH

Tank requirements

- Position: Midground to background
- Lighting: Medium to high; intense light enhances colouration
- Substrate: Adaptable; roots in both inert and nutrient-rich substrates

Maintenance & care

- Routine care: Trim tops frequently to maintain shape and encourage bushier growth; replant cuttings to fill out groupings
- Potential issues:
    - May become leggy in low light
    - Colour fades without sufficient light or iron
    - Roots shallowly; may uproot in tanks with strong flow or digging fish

PLANTS:
Epiphytes and mosses

ANUBIAS BARTERI 'NANA'

Araceae

Native habitat & ecology

- Region: West Africa
- Habitat: Shaded streams, riverbanks, and moist forest floors; often found attached to rocks or submerged wood in flowing water

Role

- Hardy, shade-tolerant epiphyte that offers visual structure, periphyton grazing surfaces, and stable cover for shrimp and bottom-dwellers without competing aggressively for nutrients.

Epiphytes and Mosses

Physical characteristics

- Form & Size: Short, horizontal rhizome with thick, dark green oval leaves; typically 5–15 cm tall
- Colour: Deep green; maintains colour in low light
- Growth Rate: Very slow; produces a new leaf every 2–3 weeks under optimal conditions

Water parameters

- Temperature: 20–28°C
- pH: 6.0–7.5
- Hardness: 2–12 dGH

Tank requirements

- Position: Foreground, midground (attached to hardscape)
- Lighting: Low to medium; high light may encourage algae growth on leaves
- Substrate: Not required; should not be buried

Maintenance & care

- Routine care: Remove yellowing leaves; wipe algae from leaf surfaces gently as needed
- Potential issues:
    - Rhizome rot if buried in substrate
    - Algae-prone in high light with low flow
    - Limited nutrient uptake due to slow growth

BOLBITIS HEUDELOTII (AFRICAN WATER FERN)

Dryopteridaceae

Native habitat & ecology

- Region: West and Central Africa
- Habitat: Shaded, slow-moving forest streams and rivers; typically found attached to rocks or submerged wood in fast-flowing sections

Role

Graceful epiphytic fern that adds vertical texture and flow-enhancing surfaces to the aquascape; provides shaded refuge for shrimp and fry while absorbing nutrients directly from the water column.

Physical characteristics

- Form & Size: Pinnate, translucent green fronds on a creeping rhizome; typically 15–40 cm tall
- Colour: Deep to bright green depending on light and nutrient levels
- Growth Rate: Slow to moderate; frond size and shape vary with flow and light conditions

Water parameters

- Temperature: 20–28°C
- pH: 6.0–7.5
- Hardness: 2–12 dGH

Tank requirements

- Position: Midground to background; attach to hardscape for optimal growth
- Lighting: Low to medium; tolerates shade but responds well to filtered light
- Substrate: Not required; should not be buried

Maintenance & care

- Routine care: Trim damaged or aged fronds; gently clean if detritus accumulates
- Potential issues:
  - Rhizome rot if buried in substrate
  - Growth stalls if there is no water movement
  - Slow to adapt after transplanting

LOMARIOPSIS CF. LINEATA (SÜSSWASSERTANG, OR FRESHWATER SEAWEED)

Lomariopsidaceae

Native habitat & ecology

- Region: Southeast Asia (Indonesia, Malaysia, Thailand)
- Habitat: Submerged growth in shaded, slow-moving tropical waters; clings to hard surfaces or forms free-floating clumps

Role

Uniquely textured liverwort-like gametophyte that provides refuge for shrimp and fry, supports microbial growth, and passively absorbs nutrients from the water column without rooting or crowding other plants.

Physical characteristics

- Form & Size: Dense, tangled mass of soft, flattened fronds resembling translucent seaweed; typically forms mounds or clumps 5–20 cm across
- Colour: Bright to medium green
- Growth Rate: Slow to moderate; spreads gradually with steady conditions

Water parameters

- Temperature: 20–28°C
- pH: 6.0–8.0
- Hardness: 0–8 dGH

Tank requirements

- Position: Foreground, hardscape, or floating; best wedged into hardscape gaps or placed in low-flow areas
- Lighting: Low to medium; retains colour in shaded tanks
- Substrate: Not required; should not be buried

Maintenance & care

- Routine care: Gently divide and reposition clumps if overgrown; rinse detritus as needed
- Potential issues:
    - May trap debris if placed in still water
    - Disintegrates under poor flow or high bioload
    - Can be mistaken for algae due to appearance

MICROSORUM PTEROPUS (JAVA FERN)

Polypodiaceae

Native habitat & ecology

- Region: Southeast Asia (Indonesia, Malaysia, Thailand)
- Habitat: Shallow streams and riverbanks; typically grows attached to rocks or wood

Role

Hardy epiphyte that provides biofilm surface for grazing species, and low-maintenance greenery for shaded areas; contributes to biological filtration by absorbing nutrients from the water column.

Epiphytes and Mosses

Physical characteristics

- Form & Size: Long, arching lance-shaped leaves from a creeping rhizome; typically 15–30 cm tall
- Colour: Medium to dark green; new leaves may appear lighter
- Growth Rate: Slow to moderate; produces new fronds regularly under stable conditions

Water parameters

- Temperature: 20–28°C
- pH: 6.0–7.5
- Hardness: 2–12 dGH

Tank requirements

- Position: Midground to background; attach to driftwood, rocks, or decorations
- Lighting: Low to medium; does well in shaded tanks
- Substrate: Not required; should not be buried

Maintenance & care

- Routine care: Remove damaged leaves; separate plantlets from leaf tips and reattach to hardscape as needed to propagate
- Potential issues:
  - Rhizome rot if buried in substrate
  - Algae may grow on leaves in high light
  - Can accumulate detritus in densely planted clumps

TAXIPHYLLUM BARBIERI (JAVA MOSS)

Hypnaceae

Native habitat & ecology

- Region: Southeast Asia (Indonesia, Malaysia, Thailand)
- Habitat: Moist tropical forests, stream banks, and submerged rocks; grows submerged or emersed in shaded, slow-moving water

Role

Fine, mat-forming moss that provides essential microhabitat for shrimp, fry, and microorganisms; traps detritus and biofilm, stabilising early-stage ecosystems and enhancing biodiversity in low-tech setups.

Epiphytes and Mosses

Physical characteristics

- Form & Size: Dense, branching filaments forming tangled mats or trailing curtains; can cover hardscape or float freely
- Colour: Bright to deep green depending on light and flow
- Growth Rate: Moderate; increases steadily with stable nutrients and gentle flow

Water parameters

- Temperature: 18–28°C
- pH: 6.0–7.5
- Hardness: 2–12 dGH

Tank requirements

- Position: Foreground, hardscape, or background mesh walls; ideal for creating natural carpets or breeding shelters
- Lighting: Low to medium; tolerates shade and indirect light
- Substrate: Not required; should not be buried

Maintenance & care

- Routine care: Trim overgrowth; remove excess detritus buildup by gently syphoning during water changes
- Potential issues:
  - May harbour excess debris if neglected
  - Can be overtaken by algae in stagnant or high-light setups
  - Difficult to fully remove once attached to surfaces

VESICULARIA MONTAGNEI (CHRISTMAS MOSS)

Hypnaceae

Native habitat & ecology

- Region: Southeast Asia (Indonesia, Philippines, Thailand)
- Habitat: Moist tropical forests, stream banks, and submerged rocks; grows submerged or emersed in shaded, slow-moving water

Role

Provides excellent shelter for shrimp, fry, and biofilm grazers while supporting surface area for beneficial bacteria. Offers a tidier appearance than Java moss and is ideal for low-tech aquascapes focused on biodiversity and visual contrast.

Physical characteristics

- Form & Size: Triangular fronds that spread horizontally in layered tiers; forms thick mats on hardscape
- Colour: Medium to dark green depending on flow and lighting
- Growth Rate: Moderate to slow; increases steadily with stable nutrients and gentle flow

Water parameters

- Temperature: 20–28°C
- pH: 5.5–7.5
- Hardness: 2–12 dGH

Tank requirements

- Position: Best attached to driftwood, rocks, or mesh; suited to foreground accents or vertical scaping
- Lighting: Low to medium; prefers indirect or diffused light
- Substrate: Not required; should not be buried

Maintenance & care

- Routine care: Trim overgrowth; remove excess detritus buildup by gently syphoning during water changes
- Potential issues:
    - Slow to recover if damaged or moved
    - Algae-prone in stagnant or overly bright tanks
    - May outcompete or smother other mosses if left unmanaged

Animals

FISH:

Centrepiece and solitary

HONEY GOURAMI

Trichogaster chuna – Osphronemidae

Native habitat & ecology

- Region: Asia (India, Bangladesh)
- Habitat: Slow-moving streams, ponds, and flooded areas; dense surface and submerged vegetation

Role

Helps manage surface biofilm and lightly grazes on plant surfaces, contributing to vegetation health without damaging delicate leaves.

Physical characteristics

- Size: 4–5 cm
- Colour variants & sexual differences: Golden-amber

colouration; males develop deeper orange/red during breeding; red/sunset and wild-type variants available
- Lifespan: 4–6 years

Water parameters

- Temperature: 22–28°C
- pH: 6.0–7.5
- Hardness: 4–15 dGH

Tank requirements

- Minimum volume: 7 US gal for a single, 10 US gal for a pair
- Planting density & types: Dense planting with floating plants and surface cover
- Lighting: Moderate; appreciates shaded areas

Behaviour & compatibility

- Schooling/social behaviour: Semi-social; not schooling but tolerant of conspecifics
- Recommended stocking number: Pairs or small groups (more females than males)
- Temperament: Peaceful; males may display to each other but rarely harmful
- Preferred swimming level: Mid to upper water levels
- Suitable tankmates: Other peaceful species; dwarf shrimp; small rasboras and tetras
- Species to avoid: Aggressive or hyperactive species; fin-nippers

Diet & feeding

- Feeding style: Omnivorous surface and mid-water feeder
- Accepted foods: Quality flake food, small pellets, frozen/live foods, vegetable matter
- Feeding tips for organic aquariums: Benefits from surface biofilm; will forage on aufwuchs (periphyton) on plant surfaces

PLAKAT BETTA

Betta splendens – Osphronemidae

Native habitat & ecology

- Region: Southeast Asia (Thailand, Cambodia, Vietnam, Laos)
- Habitat: Shallow, slow-moving waters such as rice paddies, floodplains, ditches, and swamps

Role

Surface-level predator that controls microfauna populations and biofilm, while gently grazing on soft plant surfaces in a well-planted setup.

Physical characteristics

- Size: 5–7 cm
- Colour variants & sexual differences: Wide variety including solid, koi, marble, dragon scale, and metallic hues; males exhibit brighter colours and more pronounced aggression; females are generally duller with a more rounded abdomen

Centrepiece and Solitary

- Lifespan: 2–5 years

Water parameters
- Temperature: 24–28°C
- pH: 6.5–7.5
- Hardness: 4–12 dGH

Tank requirements
- Minimum volume: 5 US gal for a single fish
- Planting density & types: Dense planting with floating plants (e.g. salvinia, Amazon frogbit) and submerged vegetation (e.g. Java fern, anubias)
- Lighting: Moderate; appreciates shaded areas and subdued lighting

Behaviour & compatibility
- Schooling/social behaviour: Solitary; males are highly territorial; females can be semi-social in sororities
- Recommended stocking number: Single male per tank; females can be kept in groups (sororities) with caution and ample space
- Temperament: Males are aggressive towards other males and similar-looking fish; females are less aggressive but still territorial
- Preferred swimming level: Top to mid-water levels
- Suitable tankmates: Peaceful, non-fin-nipping species such as Corydoras catfish, small rasboras, and snails
- Species to avoid: Other male bettas, fin-nippers, and brightly coloured or long-finned species that may trigger aggression

Diet & feeding
- Feeding style: Carnivorous surface and mid-water feeder
- Accepted foods: High-quality betta pellets, frozen/live foods like brine shrimp, bloodworms, daphnia
- Feeding tips for organic aquariums: Supplement diet with live foods to encourage natural hunting behaviour; avoid overfeeding to maintain water quality

FISH:
Schooling and social

CELESTIAL PEARL DANIO

Danio margaritatus (formerly Celestichthys margaritatus) – Cyprinidae

Native habitat & ecology
- Region: Southeast Asia (Myanmar, Thailand)
- Habitat: Small, heavily vegetated pools, often with dark substrates and partially shaded conditions

Role
Micro-predator feeding on microfauna to help regulate microorganism populations in planted tanks.

Physical characteristics
- Size: 2–2.5 cm
- Colour variants & sexual differences: Deep blue/black body with pearl-white spots and bright orange to red fins; males have more vibrant colouration and slightly slimmer bodies
- Lifespan: 3–5 years under optimal conditions

Water parameters

- Temperature: 20–26°C
- pH: 6.5–7.5
- Hardness: 2–10 dGH

Tank requirements

- Minimum volume: 10 US gal
- Planting density & types: Dense planting with abundant hiding places; moss, fine-leaved plants, and floating vegetation
- Lighting: Moderate; subdued lighting promotes natural behaviour

Behaviour & compatibility

- Schooling/social behaviour: Forms loose groups; males may establish small territories
- Recommended stocking number: 8–10 individuals minimum; displays most natural behaviour in groups
- Temperament: Peaceful but shy; needs time to acclimate to new surroundings
- Preferred swimming level: Mid to bottom levels, often among dense vegetation
- Suitable tankmates: Other small, peaceful species; dwarf shrimp; small rasboras
- Species to avoid: Larger or boisterous fish that may intimidate them

Diet & feeding

- Feeding style: Micropredator; grazes on small invertebrates
- Accepted foods: High-quality small-grained foods, frozen cyclops, daphnia, crushed flakes
- Feeding tips for organic aquariums: Multiple small feedings; benefits from mature systems with natural microorganism populations

CHERRY BARB

Rohanella titteya (formerly Puntius titteya) – Cyprinidae

Native habitat & ecology

- Region: Asia (Sri Lanka)
- Habitat: Shallow, slow-moving, and shaded streams with dense vegetation and leaf litter

Role

Contributes as a mid-water forager, grazing on small insect larvae and organic debris to support the detritus cycle of the ecosystem.

Physical characteristics

- Size: 4–5 cm
- Colour variants & sexual differences: Pronounced sexual dimorphism – males deep cherry-red, females pale gold/amber
- Lifespan: 4–6 years

Water parameters

- Temperature: 22–28°C
- pH: 6.0–7.5
- Hardness: 4–15 dGH

Tank requirements

- Minimum volume: 20 US gal
- Planting density & types: Dense planting with areas of open swimming space
- Lighting: Subdued to moderate; males show better colouration in slightly dimmed conditions

Behaviour & compatibility

- Schooling/social behaviour: Loosely shoaling; males may display to each other
- Recommended stocking number: 6–8 individuals (2 males, 4–6 females recommended)
- Temperament: Peaceful, somewhat shy
- Preferred swimming level: Mid-water, occasionally venturing to other levels
- Suitable tankmates: Other peaceful species of similar size; dwarf shrimp; peaceful bottom-dwellers
- Species to avoid: Large or aggressive species; fin-nippers

Diet & feeding

- Feeding style: Omnivorous
- Accepted foods: Quality flake food, small pellets, frozen/live foods, vegetable matter
- Feeding tips for organic aquariums: Will forage among plants and substrate for microorganisms and detritus

CHILI RASBORA

Boraras brigittae – Cyprinidae

Native habitat & ecology

- Region: Southeast Asia (Indonesia)
- Habitat: Blackwater streams, peat swamps, and marshlands with tannin-stained water

Role

Microalgae and biofilm grazer; contributes minimal waste due to small size. Their constant foraging activity helps prevent algae establishment on plant surfaces.

Physical characteristics

- Size: 1.5–2 cm
- Colour variants & sexual differences: Vibrant red with black stripe; males slightly more intensely coloured
- Lifespan: 3–5 years under optimal conditions

Water parameters

- Temperature: 22–28°C
- pH: 6.0–7.5
- Hardness: 2–12 dGH

Tank requirements

- Minimum volume: 10 US gal
- Planting density & types: Dense planting with floating plants for diffused lighting
- Lighting: Moderate to subdued; avoids bright direct light

Behaviour & compatibility

- Schooling/social behaviour: Forms loose groups; more confident in larger numbers (fewer than 6 leads to stress and hiding)
- Recommended stocking number: Add 8–12 at once to minimise stress and encourage tight shoaling
- Temperament: Peaceful but timid
- Preferred swimming level: Mid-water, often among plant thickets
- Suitable tankmates: Other small, peaceful species; dwarf shrimp; small rasboras and tetras
- Species to avoid: Larger, active fish; fin-nippers; aggressive species

Diet & feeding

- Feeding style: Micropredator/grazer
- Accepted foods: Crushed flake food, micro pellets, cyclops, vinegar eels, infusoria
- Feeding tips for organic aquariums: Multiple small feedings better than single large ones; benefits from mature systems with natural microorganism populations

EMBER TETRA

Hyphessobrycon amandae – Characidae

Native habitat & ecology

- Region: South America (Brazil – Araguaia River basin)
- Habitat: small tributaries, flooded forest areas, and blackwater streams. Abundant vegetation and leaf litter.

Role

Mid-water grazer that helps manage small insects at the water's surface while supporting nutrient cycling through active foraging.

Physical characteristics

- Size: 1.5–2 cm
- Colour variants & sexual differences: Bright orange-red body; females slightly rounder when mature
- Lifespan: 2–4 years

Schooling and Social

Water parameters

- Temperature: 22–28°C
- pH: 6.0–7.0
- Hardness: 4–12 dGH

Tank requirements

- Minimum volume: 10 US gal
- Planting density & types: Moderate to dense planting with open swimming areas
- Lighting: Moderate; adapts to various lighting conditions

Behaviour & compatibility

- Schooling/social behaviour: Active shoaling behaviour; more vibrant in groups
- Recommended stocking number: Should be kept in groups of at least 6, though larger schools are preferable for natural behaviour
- Temperament: Peaceful
- Preferred swimming level: Mid-water
- Suitable tankmates: Small peaceful species; dwarf shrimp; small rasboras
- Species to avoid: Large or predatory species; aggressive tankmates

Diet & feeding

- Feeding style: Opportunistic micropredator
- Accepted foods: Quality flake food, small pellets, frozen/live daphnia, mosquito larvae
- Feeding tips for organic aquariums: Benefits from mature systems with abundant microorganisms; avoid overfeeding

ENDLER'S LIVEBEARER

Poecilia wingei – Poeciliidae

Native habitat & ecology

- Region: South America (Venezuela)
- Habitat: Coastal lagoons, shallow streams, and drainage ditches with abundant vegetation

Role

Feeds on microfauna while contributing minimal waste. Their constant activity throughout the water column helps prevent excessive biofilm accumulation on plant surfaces.

Physical characteristics

- Size: 2.5–3.5 cm; males smaller than females
- Colour variants & sexual differences: Pronounced sexual dimorphism – males display vibrant metallic patterns in green, orange, blue, and black; females silvery-olive with subtle markings
- Lifespan: 2–3 years

Water parameters

- Temperature: 22–28°C
- pH: 6.5–8.5
- Hardness: 10–25 dGH

Tank requirements

- Minimum volume: 10 US gal
- Planting density & types: Dense planting with floating plants and cover at surface
- Lighting: Moderate; males show best colouration under good lighting

Behaviour & compatibility

- Schooling/social behaviour: Males display to females and compete with other males; females form loose groups
- Recommended stocking number: 1 male to 2–3 female ratio; groups of 8–12 minimum
- Temperament: Peaceful but active; constant movement
- Preferred swimming level: All levels with emphasis on upper half of water column
- Suitable tankmates: Small peaceful species; dwarf shrimp; non-aggressive bottom dwellers
- Species to avoid: Fin-nippers; larger predatory species; aggressive tankmates

Diet & feeding

- Feeding style: Omnivorous with preference for small live foods
- Accepted foods: Quality flake food, small pellets, frozen/live daphnia, mosquito larvae, algae
- Feeding tips for organic aquariums: Excellent foragers that will consume algae and microorganisms; multiple small feedings preserve water quality

JAPANESE RICE FISH (MEDAKA)

Oryzias latipes – Adrianichthyidae

Native habitat & ecology
- Region: East Asia (Japan – Honshu, Shikoku, Kyushu)
- Habitat: Shallow, slow-moving waters such as rice paddies, marshes, ponds, and streams; thrives among vegetation and leaf litter

Role
Predates on surface insects to support mosquito control and maintain surface activity, especially useful in outdoor or cooler setups.

Physical characteristics
- Size: 4 cm
- Colour variants & sexual differences: Wild types exhibit creamy-white to yellowish hues; captive-bred varieties

include white, creamy-yellow, orange, and transgenic colours (e.g. bright yellow, red, green). Males may display brighter colouration and more pronounced fins compared to females
- Lifespan: Typically 1–2 years in the wild; up to 3–5 years under optimal captive conditions

Water parameters

- Temperature: 10–25°C
- pH: 6.5–8.5
- Hardness: 4–20 dGH

Tank requirements

- Minimum volume: 10 US gal
- Planting density & types: Dense planting with floating plants (e.g. duckweed, frogbit) and submerged vegetation (e.g. Java moss, hornwort).
- Lighting: Moderate; appreciates natural or artificial light, with shaded areas provided by floating plants

Behaviour & compatibility

- Schooling/social behaviour: Social; thrives in groups; exhibits schooling behaviour
- Recommended stocking number: Groups of at least 6 individuals to promote natural schooling behaviour
- Temperament: Peaceful; suitable for community tanks
- Preferred swimming level: Top to mid-water levels
- Suitable tankmates: Other peaceful species such as small tetras, rasboras, guppies, and dwarf shrimp
- Species to avoid: Aggressive or predatory fish; fin-nippers

Diet & feeding

- Feeding style: Omnivorous surface feeder
- Accepted foods: High-quality flake food, micro-pellets, live or frozen foods like brine shrimp, daphnia, and mosquito larvae
- Feeding tips for organic aquariums: Benefits from natural biofilm and microorganisms present in planted tanks; supplement with appropriate-sized prepared foods

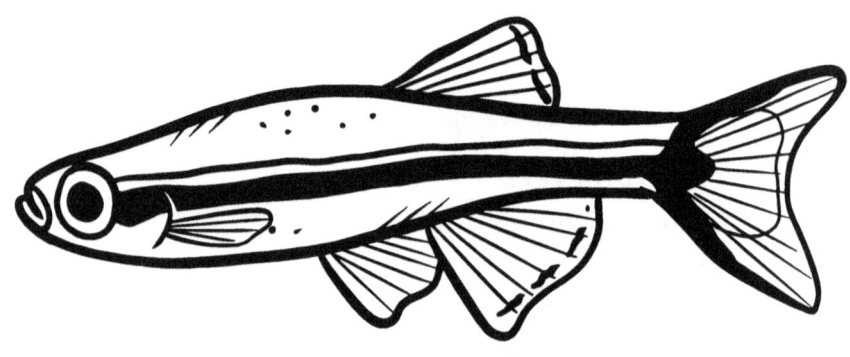

WHITE CLOUD MOUNTAIN MINNOW

Tanichthys albonubes – Cyprinidae

Native habitat & ecology

- Region: Asia (China – Guangdong Province)
- Habitat: Inhabits cool, clear streams with marginal vegetation

Role

Serves as a cool-water grazer and insect controller, feeding at the surface and mid-water zones to support balance in planted systems.

Physical characteristics

- Size: 3–4 cm
- Colour variants & sexual differences: Wild form has white/gold lateral stripe with red fins; 'gold' variant available; males have brighter colouration and slimmer bodies
- Lifespan: 3–5 years

Water parameters

- Temperature: 15–25°C
- pH: 6.0–8.0
- Hardness: 4–20 dGH

Tank requirements

- Minimum volume: 10 US gal
- Planting density & types: Moderate planting with open swimming areas
- Lighting: Moderate lighting to simulate natural conditions

Behaviour & compatibility

- Schooling/social behaviour: Forms loose aggregations rather than tight schools
- Recommended stocking number: Should be kept in groups of at least 6, though larger schools are preferable for natural behaviour
- Temperament: Peaceful, active
- Preferred swimming level: Upper to middle levels
- Suitable tankmates: Other peaceful cool-water species; cherry shrimp; peaceful bottom-dwellers
- Species to avoid: Fin-nippers; aggressive species; tropical species requiring consistently warm water

Diet & feeding

- Feeding style: Omnivorous surface and mid-water feeder
- Accepted foods: Quality flake food, small pellets, frozen/live daphnia, mosquito larvae
- Feeding tips for organic aquariums: Excellent foragers in established systems; will consume small insects that fall into the tank

FISH:
Bottom dwellers and grazers

OTOCINCLUS CATFISH

Otocinclus spp. – Loricariidae

Native habitat & ecology

- Region: South America (Brazil, Paraguay, Argentina)
- Habitat: Small streams, tributaries, and floodplains. Preference for well-oxygenated water with healthy algae growth.

Role

Specialises in grazing soft algae from plant leaves and hardscape, maintaining cleanliness without harming delicate aquatic plants.

Physical characteristics

- Size: 3–5 cm
- Colour variants & sexual differences: Typically brown/tan with a black lateral stripe; minor variations between species;

females slightly rounder when mature
- Lifespan: 3–5 years under optimal conditions

Water parameters

- Temperature: 22–26°C
- pH: 6.0–7.5
- Hardness: 4–12 dGH

Tank requirements

- Minimum volume: 10 US gal
- Planting density & types: Dense planting with broad-leaved species
- Lighting: Moderate to high; sufficient to promote some algae growth

Behaviour & compatibility

- Schooling/social behaviour: Forms loose aggregations; more active and less stressed in groups
- Recommended stocking number: 6+ individuals; social and more active in groups
- Temperament: Peaceful, somewhat shy
- Preferred swimming level: All surfaces; constantly grazes on algae
- Suitable tankmates: Other peaceful species; dwarf shrimp; small community fish
- Species to avoid: Large or aggressive species; fast-moving fish that compete for food

Diet & feeding

- Feeding style: Primarily algal grazer
- Accepted foods: Soft algae, algae wafers, blanched vegetables (courgette, spinach)
- Feeding tips for organic aquariums: Monitor carefully to ensure adequate food; may require supplemental feeding in very clean tanks

PYGMY CORYDORAS

Corydoras pygmaeus – Callichthyidae

Native habitat & ecology

- Region: South America (Brazil – Madeira River basin)
- Habitat: Slow-moving, shaded streams and tributaries with fine gravel substrates and abundant leaf litter

Role

Acts as a bottom-dwelling scavenger, consuming leftover food and organic matter to reduce waste accumulation in the substrate.

Physical characteristics

- Size: 2–3 cm
- Colour variants & sexual differences: Silvery body with dark

lateral stripe; females larger and more rounded
- Lifespan: 3–5 years

Water parameters

- Temperature: 22–26°C
- pH: 6.5–7.5
- Hardness: 4–15 dGH

Tank requirements

- Minimum volume: 10 US gal
- Planting density & types: Moderate to dense planting with open areas for foraging
- Lighting: Adaptable to various lighting conditions; prefers some shaded areas

Behaviour & compatibility

- Schooling/social behaviour: Forms loose aggregations; more active in groups
- Recommended stocking number: Minimum group of 6; more comfortable and active in larger groups
- Temperament: Peaceful
- Preferred swimming level: Bottom to mid-water; more likely to utilise water column than larger Corydoras species
- Suitable tankmates: Small peaceful species; other small catfish; dwarf shrimp
- Species to avoid: Large or aggressive species; fin-nippers

Diet & feeding

- Feeding style: Bottom-feeding omnivore
- Accepted foods: Sinking pellets and wafers, frozen/live foods, high-quality flake food
- Feeding tips for organic aquariums: Ensure food reaches the bottom; target feed if kept with more competitive species

ROSY LOACH

Petruichthys sp. 'rosy' – Nemacheilidae

Native habitat & ecology

- Region: Asia (Myanmar)
- Habitat: Shallow, slow-moving forest streams and floodplains with abundant leaf litter and vegetation

Role

Functions as an active micro-predator and detritus sifter, gently stirring the substrate while grazing on biofilm to improve substrate health.

Physical characteristics

- Size: 2.5–3.5 cm
- Colour variants & sexual differences: Males are more vividly coloured with pinkish hues and subtle iridescence; females larger, duller, and rounder
- Lifespan: 5–7 years under optimal care

Water parameters

- Temperature: 20–26 °C
- pH: 6.5–7.5
- Hardness: 4–15 dGH

Tank requirements

- Minimum volume: 20 US gal
- Planting density & types: Thrives in densely planted tanks with fine-leaved plants and leaf litter
- Lighting: Low to moderate; prefers shaded areas and subdued lighting

Behaviour & compatibility

- Schooling/social behaviour: Highly social; best kept in groups of 6 or more
- Recommended stocking number: 8+ individuals
- Temperament: Peaceful and curious; fast-moving but non-aggressive
- Preferred swimming level: Bottom to mid layer; explores plants and open substrate
- Suitable tankmates: Pygmy Corydoras, small rasboras, peaceful shrimp
- Species to avoid: Large, boisterous, or territorial species that may outcompete or harass

Diet & feeding

- Feeding style: Micro-predator and grazer
- Accepted foods: Micro pellets, crushed flakes, frozen daphnia, baby brine shrimp
- Feeding tips for organic aquariums: Benefits from live microfauna and detritus in mature soil setups; supplement with fine-quality prepared or frozen foods to support health and colour

INVERTEBRATES:
Shrimp

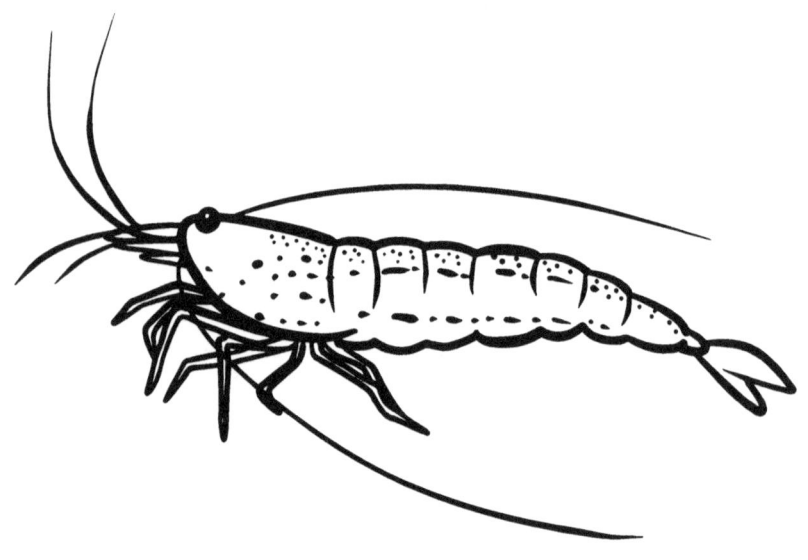

AMANO SHRIMP

Caridina multidentata (formerly Cardina japonica) – Atyidae

Native habitat & ecology

- Region: Asia (Japan, Taiwan)
- Habitat: Clear, well-oxygenated streams and rivers; rocky substrates with biofilm and algae

Role

Specialist algae controller significantly more efficient at consuming problematic algae than other invertebrates.

Physical characteristics

- Size: 4–5 cm

- Colour variants & sexual differences: Translucent body with distinctive dotted pattern; females significantly larger than males
- Lifespan: 2–3 years

Water parameters

- Temperature: 18–28°C
- pH: 6.5–8.0
- Hardness: 4–15 dGH

Tank requirements

- Minimum volume: 10 US gal
- Planting density & types: Moderate to dense planting
- Lighting: Adaptable to various lighting conditions

Behaviour & compatibility

- Schooling/social behaviour: Not schooling but more active with conspecifics
- Recommended stocking number: 3–5 individuals per 10 US gal
- Temperament: Peaceful but boldly forages and competes for food
- Preferred swimming level: All levels; constantly grazes on surfaces
- Suitable tankmates: Peaceful community fish; other shrimp; snails
- Species to avoid: Large or aggressive species; predatory species

Diet & feeding

- Feeding style: Omnivorous with strong preference for algae
- Accepted foods: Algae, biofilm, specialised shrimp foods, blanched vegetables
- Feeding tips for organic aquariums: Extremely efficient algae consumers; excellent for controlling hair algae and other problematic types

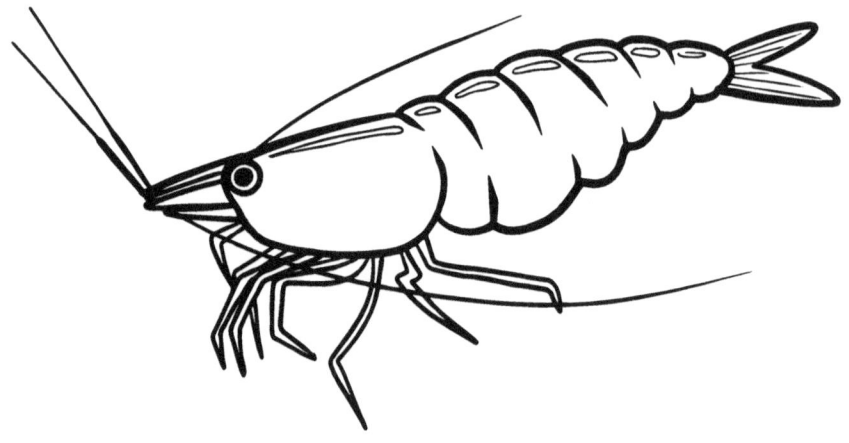

CHERRY SHRIMP

Neocaridina davidi – Atyidae

Native habitat & ecology

- Region: Asia (Taiwan, China, Korea)
- Habitat: Slow-moving streams with abundant vegetation and biofilm

Role

Primary detritivore and algae controller; processes biofilm, soft algae, and decaying plant matter.

Physical characteristics

- Size: 2–3 cm
- Colour variants & sexual differences: Numerous colour morphs including red (most common), yellow, blue, green, black, white; females larger with more rounded abdomens
- Lifespan: 1–2 years

Shrimp

Water parameters
- Temperature: 16–28°C
- pH: 6.5–8.0
- Hardness: 8–15 dGH

Tank requirements
- Minimum volume: 5 US gal
- Planting density & types: Dense planting with variety of leaf structures
- Lighting: Adaptable to various lighting conditions

Behaviour & compatibility
- Schooling/social behaviour: Not schooling but thrives in colonies
- Recommended stocking number: 10+ individuals for breeding colony
- Temperament: Peaceful
- Preferred swimming level: Primarily bottom to mid-water; grazes on all surfaces
- Suitable tankmates: Small peaceful fish; other dwarf shrimp of similar size; snails
- Species to avoid: Most fish will prey on shrimplets; avoid larger opportunistic feeders

Diet & feeding
- Feeding style: Omnivorous grazer
- Accepted foods: Biofilm, algae, specialised shrimp foods, blanched vegetables, leaf litter
- Feeding tips for organic aquariums: Rarely *need* supplemental feeding, but including blanched vegetables and high-quality specialty shrimp food will benefit colonies.

INVERTEBRATES:
Snails

MALAYSIAN TRUMPET SNAIL

Melanoides tuberculata – Thiaridae

Native habitat & ecology
- Region: Southeast Asia; now widespread across the globe
- Habitat: Streams, rivers, lakes, and ponds with soft substrates for burrowing

Role
Substrate aerator and detritus processor; burrows through soil and sand, preventing compaction and anaerobic zones. Their continuous movement helps cycle nutrients and prevents toxic buildup in the substrate.

Physical characteristics
- Size: 2–3 cm

- Colour variants & sexual differences: Conical spiral shell in brown/tan colouration with darker spots; minimal variation
- Lifespan: 1–2 years

Water parameters

- Temperature: 20–30°C
- pH: 6.5–8.0
- Hardness: 5–20 dGH

Tank requirements

- Minimum volume: 1 US gal
- Planting density & types: Not dependent on planting density
- Lighting: Primarily nocturnal; lighting not a significant factor

Behaviour & compatibility

- Schooling/social behaviour: Solitary; no social requirements
- Recommended stocking number: Start with 3–5 individuals; population will self-regulate based on available food
- Temperament: Peaceful
- Preferred level: Primarily substrate-dwelling; most active at night
- Suitable tankmates: Most community fish; shrimp; other peaceful species
- Species to avoid: Snail-eating species such as loaches, puffers, and assassin snails

Diet & feeding

- Feeding style: Detritivore and substrate sifter
- Accepted foods: Primarily consumes detritus, decaying plant matter, and uneaten fish food
- Feeding tips for organic aquariums: Rarely needs supplemental feeding in established tanks; particularly valuable in tanks with soil substrates

NERITE SNAIL

Neritina natalensis – Neritidae

Native habitat & ecology

- Region: East Africa; found in brackish and freshwater habitats worldwide
- Habitat: Streams, rivers, and lake shorelines with algae-covered rocks

Role

Specialist algae consumer and glass cleaner; particularly effective at removing green spot algae from hard surfaces.

Physical characteristics

- Size: 1–2.5 cm
- Colour variants & sexual differences: Multiple species and

colour patterns available; zebra, tiger, black, and horned varieties common
- Lifespan: 1–2 years

Water parameters

- Temperature: 18–28°C
- pH: 6.5–8.5
- Hardness: 8–20 dGH

Tank requirements

- Minimum volume: 3 US gal
- Planting density & types: Not dependent on planting density
- Lighting: Not dependent on lighting conditions

Behaviour & compatibility

- Schooling/social behaviour: Solitary; no social requirements
- Recommended stocking number: 1 per 3 US gal as a general guideline
- Temperament: Peaceful
- Preferred swimming level: Primarily on hard surfaces; glass, rocks, driftwood
- Suitable tankmates: Most community fish; shrimp; other peaceful species
- Species to avoid: Snail-eating species like puffers and certain loaches

Diet & feeding

- Feeding style: Algae grazer
- Accepted foods: Primarily consumes algae; rarely accepts prepared foods
- Feeding tips for organic aquariums: Rarely needs supplemental feeding in established tanks; may require calcium supplement in very soft water

RAMSHORN SNAIL

Planorbidae family (various species) – Planorbidae

Native habitat & ecology
- Region: Global distribution; found on every continent except Antarctica
- Habitat: Still or slow-moving freshwater including ponds, lakes, and streams with abundant surfaces for grazing

Role
Primary algae controller and detritus processor; excels at consuming soft surface algae and organic debris that would otherwise decompose and affect water quality.

Physical characteristics
- Size: 2.5 cm

Snails

- Colour variants & sexual differences: Available in multiple colours including red, blue, brown, gold, pink, and leopard-spotted patterns; no visible sexual differences (hermaphroditic)
- Lifespan: 1–1.5 years under optimal conditions

Water parameters

- Temperature: 20–26°C
- pH: 7.0–8.0
- Hardness: 8–20 dGH

Tank requirements

- Minimum volume: 1 US gal
- Planting density & types: Benefits from abundant surfaces including plants, hardscape, and glass
- Lighting: Any lighting sufficient to grow algae

Behaviour & compatibility

- Schooling/social behaviour: Solitary; no social requirements
- Recommended stocking number: Start with 3–5 individuals; population will self-regulate based on available food
- Temperament: Peaceful
- Preferred swimming level: Surfaces throughout the tank including glass, plants, and hardscape
- Suitable tankmates: Most peaceful fish and invertebrates
- Species to avoid: Snail-eating species such as loaches, puffers, and assassin snails

Diet & feeding

- Feeding style: Constant grazer using radula to scrape surfaces
- Accepted foods: Primarily consumes soft algae, biofilm, detritus, and leftover fish food
- Feeding tips for organic aquariums: Rarely needs supplemental feeding in established tanks; population will naturally adjust to available food sources

Microfauna

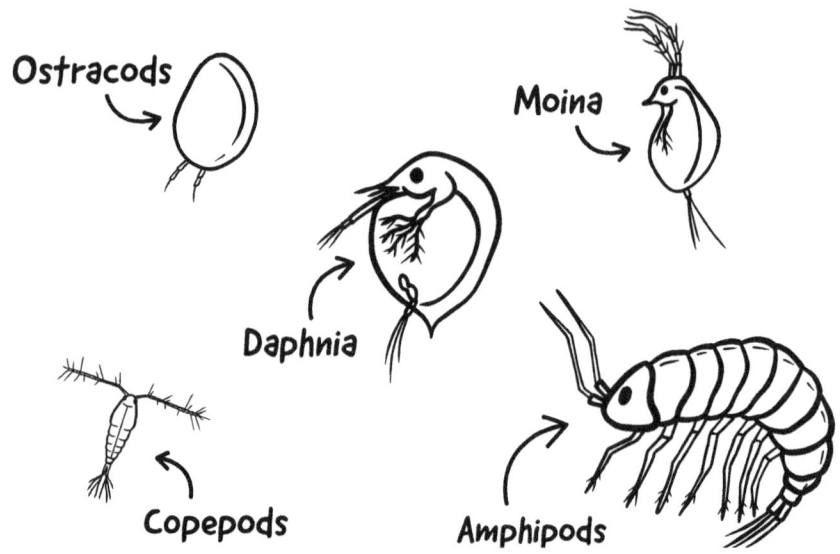

CRUSTACEANS

Various families – Copepoda, Cladocera, Ostracoda, Amphipoda

Includes

- Copepods, daphnia, moina, ostracods (seed shrimp), amphipods (scuds)

Role

This group includes filter feeders (e.g. daphnia, moina) and detritivores (e.g. copepods, ostracods, amphipods). These tiny invertebrates recycle waste, graze algae, and provide natural live food for fry and small fish. Their presence is a hallmark of microbial richness and system maturity.

Physical characteristics

- Size: 0.3–5 mm depending on species
- Form: Jumping (copepods), seed-shaped (ostracods), swimming/floating (daphnia), or shrimp-like (amphipods)
- Lifespan: Days to weeks; reproduce quickly and in large numbers

Water parameters

- Temperature: 18–28°C
- pH: 6.5–8.0
- Hardness: 5–18 dGH

Diet & feeding

- Feeding style: Filter feeders, detritivores, algae grazers
- Accepted foods: Bacteria, microalgae, biofilm, detritus
- Feeding tips: No direct feeding needed; populations adjust to natural food levels

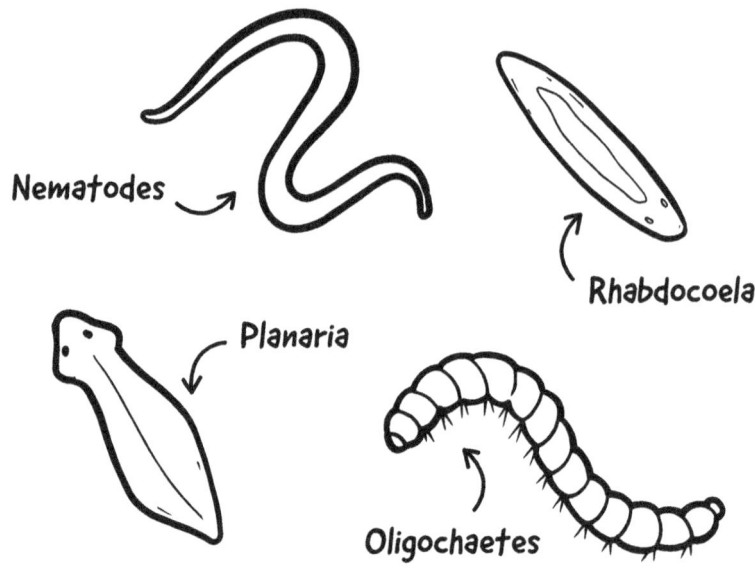

WORMS

Various families – Nematoda, Annelida, Platyhelminthes

Includes
- Nematodes, oligochaetes (detritus worms), planaria, rhabdocoela

Role
Worms play a foundational role in the detrital food web. Nematodes and oligochaetes break down organic waste and help aerate the soil. Flatworms like rhabdocoela help balance microbial populations. Most worms are harmless and self-regulating, with population size reflecting nutrient availability.

Microfauna

Physical characteristics

- Size: 0.2–10 mm depending on species
- Form: Thread-like (nematodes), segmented (oligochaetes), flat and gliding (planaria)
- Lifespan: Weeks to months; reproduce rapidly in favourable conditions

Water parameters

- Temperature: 18–28°C
- pH: 6.0–8.0
- Hardness: 3–15 dGH

Diet & feeding

- Feeding style: Detritivores, micro-predators, and grazers
- Accepted foods: Bacteria, biofilm, decaying organic matter
- Feeding tips: No feeding required; populations naturally adjust to available waste

PLANARIA WARNING: In high numbers, planaria can prey on shrimp or eggs.

SAFE PLANARIA REMOVAL TIPS:

- Manual removal: Siphon during water changes or extract using fine tweezers
- Use traps: Bait glass tubes or mesh containers with shrimp pellets overnight
- Control feeding: Reducing excess food will limit reproduction
- Avoid crushing: If squashed into multiple segments, planaria may regenerate
- Use natural predators: Some predatory fish may help control populations

OTHER: FRESHWATER LIMPETS

Limpets Ferrissia spp. – Ancylidae (Mollusca)

Role

Tiny, harmless grazers that resemble flat snails. Limpets feed on soft algae and biofilm without harming plants or glass.

Physical characteristics

- Size: 1–3 mm
- Form: Flattened, translucent dome with a muscular foot
- Lifespan: Up to 1 year

Water parameters

- Temperature: 18–26°C
- pH: 6.5–8.0
- Hardness: 6–20 dGH

Diet & feeding

- Feeding style: Surface grazer
- Accepted foods: Biofilm, soft algae
- Feeding tips: No feeding needed; populations remain low in clean systems

HYDRA SPP.

Hydra Hydra spp. – Cnidaria

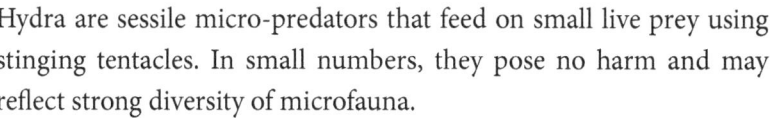

Role

Hydra are sessile micro-predators that feed on small live prey using stinging tentacles. In small numbers, they pose no harm and may reflect strong diversity of microfauna.

> **HYDRA WARNING:** In large numbers, hydra may sting fry or shrimp larvae. Monitor closely in breeding tanks.

Physical characteristics

- Size: 1–5 mm
- Form: Cylindrical body with 4–8 waving tentacles
- Lifespan: Weeks to months; reproduce rapidly via budding

Water parameters

- Temperature: 18–26°C
- pH: 6.5–8.0
- Hardness: 4–15 dGH

Diet & feeding

- Feeding style: Passive ambush predator
- Accepted foods: Copepods, daphnia, infusoria, fry
- Feeding tips: No feeding needed in tanks with natural microfauna

Notes

BIBLIOGRAPHY

EPIGRAPH

'*Spring becomes stream becomes river, and all three seek the sea.*': Is a River Alive? by Robert Macfarlane (Penguin, Hamish Hamilton); reproduced by permission of David Higham Associates.

ENDNOTES

1. Walstad, *Ecology of the Planted Aquarium*.
2. Adey, *Dynamic Aquaria*.
3. Adey, *Dynamic Aquaria*.
4. Odum and Heald, 'The Detritus-Based Food Web of an Estuarine Mangrove Community'.
5. Lowenfels, *Teaming with Microbes*.
6. Hiscock, *Encyclopedia of Aquarium Plants*.
7. Randall, *Sunken Gardens*.
8. Gross et al., 'Soil Nitrifying Enrichments as Biofilter Starters in Intensive Recirculating Saline Water Aquaculture'.
9. Walstad, *Ecology of the Planted Aquarium*.
10. Walstad, *Ecology of the Planted Aquarium*.
11. Hiscock, *Encyclopedia of Aquarium Plants*.
12. Randall, *Sunken Gardens*.
13. Randall, *Sunken Gardens*.
14. i4x4nMore, 'PAR Data-Spiral Power Saver Bulbs, Lighting Question'.
15. Walstad, *Ecology of the Planted Aquarium*.
16. Hiscock, *Encyclopedia of Aquarium Plants*.
17. Walstad, *Ecology of the Planted Aquarium*.
18. Adey, *Dynamic Aquaria*.
19. Hiscock, *Encyclopedia of Aquarium Plants*.
20. Walstad, *Ecology of the Planted Aquarium*.
21. Walstad, *Ecology of the Planted Aquarium*.
22. Lowenfels, *Teaming with Microbes*.
23. Talbot, 'How-To: Mineralized Soil Substrate'.
24. Hiscock, *Encyclopedia of Aquarium Plants*.
25. Walstad, *Ecology of the Planted Aquarium*.

26 Walstad, *Ecology of the Planted Aquarium.*
27 Wetzel, *Wetzel's Limnology.*
28 Walstad, *Ecology of the Planted Aquarium.*
29 Walstad, *Ecology of the Planted Aquarium.*
30 Hiscock, *Encyclopedia of Aquarium Plants.*
31 Witynski, 'What Is Ecological Succession?'
32 Ponnamperuma, 'Some Aspects of the Physical Chemistry of Paddy Soils'.
33 Lowenfels, *Teaming with Microbes.*

BIBLIOGRAPHY

Adey, Walter H. *Dynamic Aquaria: Building and Restoring Ecosystems and the Biosphere.* Fourth edition. Academic Press, 2024.

Gross, Amit, Anna Nemirovsky, Dina Zilberg, et al. 'Soil Nitrifying Enrichments as Biofilter Starters in Intensive Recirculating Saline Water Aquaculture'. *Aquaculture* 223, no. 1 (2003): 51–62. https://doi.org/10.1016/S0044-8486(03)00067-X.

Hiscock, Peter. *Encyclopedia of Aquarium Plants.* De Vecchi Ediciones, 2024.

i4x4nMore. 'PAR Data-Spiral Power Saver Bulbs, Lighting Question'. The Planted Tank Forum, 31 March 2008. https://www.plantedtank.net/threads/par-data-spiral-power-saver-bulbs-lighting-question.85667/.

Lowenfels, Jeff. *Teaming with Microbes: The Organic Gardener's Guide to the Soil Food Web.* Rev. ed. With Wayne Lewis. Timber Press, 2010.

Odum, William E., and Eric J. Heald. 'The Detritus-Based Food Web of an Estuarine Mangrove Community'. In *Estuarine Research*, edited by George E. Cronin, vol. 1. Academic Press, 1975.

Ponnamperuma, F. N. 'Some Aspects of the Physical Chemistry of Paddy Soils'. *Proceedings of Symposium on Paddy Soils* (Berlin, Heidelberg), Springer, 1981, 59–94. https://doi.org/10.1007/978-3-642-68141-7_5.

Randall, Karen A. *Sunken Gardens: A Step-by-Step Guide to Planting Freshwater Aquariums.* Timber Press, 2016.

Notes

Talbot, Aaron. 'How-To: Mineralized Soil Substrate'. Aquatic Plant Forum. Accessed 9 July 2025. https://www.aquaticplantcentral.com/threads/how-to-mineralized-soil-substrate-by-aaron-talbot.52554/.

Walstad, Diana Louise. *Ecology of the Planted Aquarium: A Practical Manual and Scientific Treatise*. Echinodorus Pub, 2023.

Wetzel, Robert G. *Wetzel's Limnology: Lake and River Ecosystems*. Fourth edition. Edited by I. D. Jones and J. P. Smol. Academic Press, an imprint of Elsevier, 2024.

Witynski, Max. 'What Is Ecological Succession? | University of Chicago News'. Accessed 12 July 2025. https://news.uchicago.edu/explainer/what-is-ecological-succession.

RESOURCES

BOOKS & PUBLICATIONS

Coletti, Ted. The Tub Pond Handbook: The Comprehensive Guide to Patio Ponds, Container Water Gardens, and Taking Your Aquarium Hobby Outside. 3rd ed. Wagtail Imprints, Inc., 2021.

Farmer, George. Aquascaping: A Step-by-Step Guide to Planting, Styling, and Maintaining Beautiful Aquariums. Simon and Schuster, 2020.

Fritz, Uwe. Medaka: Japanese Rice Fish. Self-published, 2021.

Hiscock, Peter. Encyclopedia of Aquarium Plants. De Vecchi Ediciones, 2024.

James, Richard. Neocaridina Shrimp Handbook: A Complete Guide to Cherry Shrimp. Self-published, 2024.

Kasselmann, Christel. Aquarium Plants: A Colour Atlas. English ed. Self-published, 2020.

Lowenfels, Jeff, and Wayne Lewis. Teaming with Microbes: The Organic Gardener's Guide to the Soil Food Web. Revised ed. Timber Press, 2010.

Newell, Ben. Hello Tiny World: An Enchanting Journey into the World of Creating Terrariums. Dorling Kindersley, 2024.

Randall, Karen A. Sunken Gardens: A Step-by-Step Guide to Planting Freshwater Aquariums. Timber Press, 2017.

Strietman, Tai. Aquatic Habitats: Aquariums Inspired by Nature. Skyhorse Publishing. 2025.

Walstad, Diana L. Ecology of the Planted Aquarium: A Practical Manual and Scientific Treatise for the Home Aquarist. 4th ed. Echinodorus Publishing, 2023.

FORUMS & ONLINE COMMUNITIES

Aquarium Co-op Forum (*https://forum.aquariumcoop.com/*) – Multiple threads featuring user-submitted soil-based setups.

Aquatic Plant Central (*https://www.aquaticplantcentral.com/*) – Multiple threads discussing substrate microbiology and plant health.

Barr Report (*https://www.barrreport.com*) – Dr. Tom Barr's extensive archive of articles and forum discussions on planted tank nutrient management, including threads related to soil-based aquariums.

The Planted Tank Forum (*https://www.plantedtank.net/*) – Dedicated "Walstad Method" and "Planted Nano Tanks" subforums for specific advice.

UK Aquatic Plant Society Forum (*https://www.ukaps.org/*) – Specialist society discussions on temperate and tropical soil-based tanks.

IN-DEPTH WEB GUIDES & TUTORIALS

Betta Botanicals® (*https://bettabotanicals.com/*) – Comprehensive resource for botanical method aquariums, including organic-substrate experiments.

Phillips Fish Works (*https://www.phillipsfishworks.com/*) - Insightful resources on the role of microorganisms in your aquarium.

Tannin Aquatics (*https://www.tanninaquatics.com*) – Scott Fellman's The Tint blog includes case studies on blackwater style and botanical method aquariums, including organic-substrate experiments.

Wild Aquarist (*https://wildaquarist.com/*) – Offers clear, engaging guides to betta care with an emphasis on balance and beginner-friendly design.

Notes

YOUTUBE CHANNELS

Aquarium Co-Op (*@aquariumcoop*) – Offers comprehensive, in-depth videos on plant and animal care, equipment, and low-tech aquarium setups.

BioLilianne (*@BioLilianne*) – Explores natural aquariums and aquatic plants with a focus on low-tech methods.

Bucket Ponds (*@BucketPonds*) – Dedicated to outdoor bucket ponds and container water gardens, demonstrating natural ecosystem cycles.

The Cine Scaper (*@TheCineScaper*) – Cinematic, plant-focused aquascaping tutorials and nature-inspired tank builds with beautiful visuals.

EC Scapes (*@ecscapes*) – Offers beautifully planted aquariums that demonstrate how thoughtful design and healthy plants can create a natural system.

Fish Shop Matt (*@FishShopMatt*) – Practical, hobbyist-focused builds, fish room tours, and low-tech planted setups with an easy-going style.

FISHTORY (*@Fishtory*) - A passionate exploration of aquariums as ecosystems, showing what works (and what doesn't) when you let nature lead.

Foo the Flowerhorn (*@FootheFlowerhorn*) – Features a multi-year observation series of soil-based aquariums tracking ecosystem health.

George Farmer Studios (*@GeorgeFarmerStudios*) – Aquarium builds, workshops, and insights into nature-inspired aquascaping.

GlassBoxDiaries (*@GlassBoxDiaries*) – Myth-busting series on misconceptions and hands-on soil-based aquarium builds.

Haus of Gruen (*@hausofgruen*) – Stylish aquascaping with a modern aesthetic, blending natural aquarium techniques with artistic presentation.

Julia Zuskey (*@juliazuskey*) – Chronicles a detailed Walstad build with extended plant growth and observations.

Jurijs Jutjajevs (*@JurijsJutjajevs*) – Shares practical aquascaping tips and thoughtful insights into building stable, planted aquariums.

KeepingFishSimple (*@KeepingFishSimple*) – Beginner-friendly guides to low-tech planted tanks, shrimp, and fish care.

Lindsay's Tanks (*@lindsaystanks*) – Hidden gem! Low-tech aquarium videos which are passionately produced with amazing visuals.

How to Create an Organic Aquarium

MD Fish Tanks (@*MDFishTanks*) – High-production aquascaping tutorials that include low-tech soil setups and ecosystem-based builds.

MJ Aquascaping (@*MJAquascaping*) – Creative nature aquarium tutorials, design journeys, and clear step-by-step builds.

Peace of Nature (@*peaceofnaturee*) – Demonstrates long-term, low-tech aquariums with a commitment to natural processes.

Roots, Reefs & Reactions (@*RootsReefsandReactions*) – Approachable and candid look at soil-based aquariums through a scientific lens.

SerpaDesign (@*SerpaDesign*) – Focused on terrariums and paludariums but includes fantastic natural aquascape builds.

Shiny Scales with Owen (@*shinyscalesmedia*) – Fun approach with a curious exploration of aquatic ecosystems and DIY builds.

ShrimpKeepingAnswers (@*ShrimpKeepingAnswers*) – Focused, beginner-friendly advice on Neocaridina shrimp care, tank setup, and breeding.

sm9llfish (@*sm9llfish*) – Quick, inspiring Walstad-method clips showcasing small-scale organic aquarium successes.

tanks for nothin (@*tanksfornothin*) – Creative, budget-friendly, DIY builds that mirror organic, soil-based aquarium minimalism.

Terrarium Designs (@*TerrariumDesigns*) – Focused on lush terrarium and paludarium builds, with standout videos on natural shrimp tanks.

Tiny Menagerie (@*tinymenagerie*) – Provides expert nano-animal keeping and micro-ecosystem care tutorials. I cannot recommend this channel enough!

The Urban Nemophilist (@*TheUrbanNemophilist*) – Hands-on builds, showcasing natural aquarium keeping in beautifully filmed segments.

Walstad Method Step by Step (@*walstadmethodstepbystep*) – Dedicated channel guiding viewers through each stage of a no-CO_2, no-filter dirted setup.

Worcester Terrariums (@*worcesterterrariums*) – Showcases beautifully crafted terrariums that blend art, ecology, and storytelling.

World of Whasian (@*WorldofWhasian*) – A candid channel that shares low-tech aquariums. Ideal for learners who enjoy growing alongside the process.

UNIT CONVERSIONS

LITRES	US GALLONS
4	1
9	2.5
19	5
38	10
57	15
76	20
114	30
151	40
189	50
208	55
284	75
379	100
454	120
681	180

HARDNESS	dGH	ppm
Very Soft	0 – 4	0 – 70
Soft	4 – 8	70 – 140
Medium	8 – 12	140 – 210
Hard	12 – 18	210 – 320
Very Hard	18 – 30	320 – 530

CENTIMETRES (CM)	INCHES (")
0.5	0.20
1.0	0.39
1.5	0.59
2.0	0.79
2.5	0.98
3.0	1.18
3.5	1.38
4.0	1.58
4.5	1.77
5.0	1.97
10.0	3.94
15.0	5.91
20.0	7.87
25.0	9.84
30.0	11.81
35.0	13.78
40.0	15.75
45.0	17.72
50.0	19.69
60.0	23.62
70.0	27.56
80.0	31.50
90.0	35.43
100.0	39.37

Notes

CELCIUS	FAHRENHEIT
30	86
28	82.4
26	78.8
24	75.2
22	71.6
20	68
18	64.4
16	60.8
14	57.2
12	53.6
10	50
8	46.4
6	42.8
4	39.2
2	35.6
0	32

Acknowledgements

CONTRIBUTORS

This book was shaped by the generous community of hobbyists, creators, and writers who have shared their experiences. In particular, I want to thank the people who have given me their time and attention to improve this book. Their thoughtful feedback helped sharpen the clarity and usefulness throughout:

Adam from *Dirty Roots*

Alex from *FISHTORY*

Alex from *World of Whasian*

Ben from *Betta Botanicals®*

Edward from *EC Scapes*

Fur from *Wild Aquarist*

Harris from *Pond Life Aquatics*

Jonas from *Haus of Gruen*

Justin from *Tropiscape Aquatics*

Kyle from *Roofs, Reefs, and Reactions*

Mohib from *Urban Farmer*

Nestor from *HabitatForge*

Peter from *Walstad Method Step by Step*

How to Create an Organic Aquarium

Phai from *Gentle Ficus*

Shaun from *Glass Box Diaries*

Sushanto from *The Urban Nemophilist*

tanks for nothin

Lastly, I want to thank Sophie, an amazing editor and an even better friend. Her honest judgement and sharp eye brought structure to chaos. And she has a greener thumb than anyone I've ever known. I'm envious.

Their insights shaped the work; any errors are my own.

With appreciation,

Oli

P.S. And of course to Gumnut the Grumpy Gourami, my ever-watchful companion. Thank you for tolerating the many homes I've built you as I indulge this obsession. Your judgemental stare keeps me in my place.

Gumnut

If this book helped you, please consider sharing your experience through an honest rating or review. When readers share their thoughts on Amazon, it helps the platform understand who benefits most from this content, connecting the book with more curious aquarists just like you. You can leave a review in under a minute by scanning this code with your phone camera.

ABOUT THE AUTHOR

OLIVER JAMIESON is a furniture maker from the north of England. His interest in nature started early thanks to his parents. A childhood spent in the garden, in the woods, out fishing, out hiking, and many laps around the field with four springer spaniels have made Oli who he is today. He lives with his wife in the East Riding of Yorkshire.

www.ingramcontent.com/pod-product-compliance
Lightning Source LLC
Chambersburg PA
CBHW031147020426
42333CB00013B/554